The Done List for Loved Ones

How to Support Someone with Anxiety Without Losing Yourself

Angie G. Ford

Sunflower Phoenix Publishing

ISBN: 979-8-9959413-2-3

Published by Sunflower Phoenix Publishing

Note to Reader

This book is not a substitute for professional mental health care. If anxiety is severe, worsening, or connected to thoughts of self-harm, seek help from a qualified professional or crisis service immediately.

For the ones who stay.

For the partners, the parents, and the friends who sit in the quiet rooms,
who learn a new language of safety,
and who hold the light steady
while the people they love find their way back to the world.

Table of Contents

Chapter 1: What Anxiety Can Look Like From the Outside

1. The Confusion of the Outside View

If you are reading this book, you are likely exhausted. You love someone who is struggling with severe anxiety, and you have probably spent months or even years trying to help them. You have offered advice, you have taken over their chores, you have adjusted your schedule, and you have tried to be as patient as humanly possible.

And yet, nothing seems to be working.

Before we talk about what anxiety is, we need to validate what it feels like to be you right now. It is incredibly confusing. It is deeply frustrating. And if you are being entirely honest with yourself, you might be carrying a quiet, heavy resentment that you feel terribly guilty about.

You feel this way because, from the outside, anxiety rarely looks the way you expect it to. If you are waiting to see someone trembling, hyperventilating, or visibly panicked in a corner, you might miss what is actually happening right in front of you. What loved ones usually see is something much quieter, much more baffling, and much easier to misinterpret.

You see a highly capable person who suddenly cannot do simple things.

You know how smart they are. You know how much they have accomplished in the past. You might have watched them handle major life crises, manage complex work projects, or navigate difficult family dynamics with grace. So when you walk into the kitchen and see them staring blankly at a small pile of laundry, or when they spend three days avoiding a basic phone call to the dentist, it simply does not compute. The math does not work. How can someone who is so competent fall apart over deciding what to make for dinner?

2. Five Scenarios: The Freeze in Real Life

The disconnect between their past capability and their current paralysis is where the frustration breeds. Basic tasks are left undone, and those tasks seem incredibly easy from the outside. Let us look at five common scenarios to see how this disconnect plays out in real time.

<u>Scenario 1:</u> The Unanswered Texts

What you see: They have four unread text messages from good friends. The messages are simple ("Hey, how are you?"), but they have left them on 'read' for a week. They are still scrolling social media, but they will not reply to the texts.

What you assume: They are being rude. They are ignoring people who care about them. They are perfectly capable of typing on their phone, so they must just not want to talk to anyone.

What is really happening: They want to reply, but they feel like they have to craft the "perfect" response to prove they are doing well. The pressure to sound normal is so high that they freeze. The longer they wait, the more ashamed they feel for ignoring their friends, which makes replying even harder.

Mishandled response: "Why haven't you texted Sarah back? It takes two seconds. You're being rude." (This adds shame and guarantees they will not text back today.)

Handled-well response: "I know texting feels like a lot of pressure right now. Do you want me to text Sarah and just tell her we're having a quiet week?"

Why this works: This removes the pressure entirely. It validates the hidden difficulty they are facing without judging them for it. By offering to bridge the gap, you show that you are on their team, and you give their nervous system permission to rest without the heavy burden of social performance.

Scenario 2: Shower Avoidance

What you see: They have been in the same clothes for two days. The bathroom is ten feet away, the water is hot, but they cannot seem to initiate the process of getting in. They are sitting on the couch watching TV instead.

What you assume: They have given up. They are being lazy. They do not care about their hygiene or how it affects the household.

What is really happening: The executive function required to transition from "sitting" to "showering" is completely offline. A shower is not one step; it is twenty steps (getting up, finding clothes, turning on water, adjusting temperature, undressing, washing, drying, dressing). To an exhausted nervous system, twenty steps feels like climbing a mountain.

Mishandled response: "You really need to take a shower. You've been on the couch all day." (This induces deep shame and reinforces their feeling of brokenness.)

Handled-well response: "Hey, I'm going to start the shower water for you and put a clean towel on the counter. No rush, just whenever you're ready."

Why this works: This removes the transition friction and lowers the barrier to entry. You are not demanding action; you are simply setting the stage for it. By removing the initial steps of the process, you make the mountain look a little more like a small hill.

<u>Scenario 3:</u> Canceled Plans

What you see: You both agreed to go to a friend's house for dinner. They seemed excited about it yesterday. But an hour before it is time to leave, they suddenly declare that they cannot go, retreating to the bedroom and leaving you to awkwardly text the host.

What you assume: They are manipulative. They waited until the last minute on purpose. They are making your life harder and ruining your social life.

What is really happening: The thought of sitting in a room full of people, masking their panic, and pretending to be okay suddenly felt like a physical impossibility. Their body entered a fight-or-flight state. They canceled to protect themselves from a public meltdown, and now they are drowning in guilt for ruining your evening.

Mishandled response: "You do this every time. I can't believe you're bailing on me again. Fine, I'll just go by myself." (This confirms their fear that they are a burden.)

Handled-well response: "Okay, we don't have to go. Your nervous system is saying no today, and that's fine. I'll text them and handle it. Let's just stay in."

Why this works: This prioritizes their safety over the social obligation. It communicates that their well-being is more important to you than attending the dinner. This kind of response builds deep trust, showing them that you will not punish them for something their body is forcing them to do.

Scenario 4: The Unopened Mail

What you see: There is a stack of mail on the kitchen counter that has been sitting there for three weeks. They walk past it every day, sometimes even moving it to wipe the counter, but they never open a single envelope.

What you assume: They are being completely irresponsible. They expect you to manage all the adult tasks in the house, and they are intentionally ignoring their financial or personal obligations.

What is really happening: To an anxious brain, an unopened envelope is not just paper. It is a potential disaster. It could be a bill they cannot pay, a mistake they made, or a demand they do not have the energy to meet. Leaving it unopened keeps the disaster as a "maybe" rather than a "definitely." Opening it feels like stepping onto a landmine.

Mishandled response: "Are you ever going to open your mail? I am not your secretary. You need to act like an adult and deal with this." (This spikes their panic and makes the mail feel even more dangerous.)

Handled-well response: "I noticed the mail is piling up. Would it help if I sat with you while you open it, or do you want me to sort through it and just tell you if there is anything urgent?"

Why this works: This acknowledges the fear without mocking it. By offering to act as a buffer between them and the potential "disaster" inside the envelopes, you reduce the perceived threat level. You are offering a safe bridge over a terrifying gap.

<u>Scenario 5:</u> The Kitchen Stare / Can't Choose Food

What you see: They are standing in front of the open refrigerator. They have been standing there for five minutes. The fridge is full of food, but they eventually close the door with a sigh and walk away without eating anything.

What you assume: They are being overly picky. They are waiting for you to offer to cook something for them, or they are just trying to be difficult.

What is really happening: They are experiencing severe decision fatigue. Anxiety consumes an enormous amount of mental energy, leaving very little fuel for basic choices. Deciding what to eat requires evaluating options, considering preparation time, and anticipating how the food will make them feel. Right now, their brain cannot process those variables. The effort required to choose is greater than the sensation of hunger.

Mishandled response: "The fridge is completely full. Just pick something and eat. Stop being so dramatic about a sandwich." (This dismisses their cognitive overload and makes them feel foolish.)

Handled-well response: "Decision fatigue is hitting hard today, isn't it? I am going to make some toast. I will make you a piece too, and I will just leave it on the counter."

Why this works: This bypasses the need for them to make a choice entirely. You are recognizing that their executive function is tapped out, and you are providing nourishment without requiring them to spend any mental energy to get it.

3. Common Misreads

Because the behavior makes no logical sense, your brain tries to fill in the gaps. When you are tired and stressed yourself, you naturally interpret their behavior through the lens of your own frustration. This leads to a set of very common, very destructive assumptions.

Common Misread:
"They are being lazy."

What is actually happening:
They are frozen. Their nervous system is overloaded. Sitting on the couch scrolling looks like laziness, but it is often a desperate attempt to distract a racing mind. When you assume laziness, you assume a lack of moral character. But a freeze response is a biological event, not a character flaw. They are not choosing to avoid work; their body is preventing them from starting it.

Common Misread:
"They are being rude."

What is actually happening:
They are overloaded. Snapping at you or ignoring a question is rarely about you. It is usually because their brain cannot process one more piece of sensory input. If you take their short answers personally, you will end up in a fight over their tone of voice, completely missing the fact that they are drowning in internal noise.

Common Misread:
"They are manipulative."

What is actually happening:
They have inconsistent capacity. A good day does not prove a hard day is fake. Their ability to function

fluctuates wildly based on internal noise you cannot hear. It is easy to feel tricked when they are fine on Tuesday but paralyzed on Wednesday. However, this inconsistency is the hallmark of an anxious nervous system, not a master plan to control you.

Common Misread:
"They don't care."

What is actually happening:
They care too much. Avoidance is often driven by intense perfectionism and a terrifying fear of doing the task wrong or letting you down. They would rather do nothing than do it imperfectly and face your disappointment. Their inaction is actually a twisted form of caring deeply about the outcome.

Common Misread:
"They are doing this on purpose."

What is actually happening:
They are in survival mode. No one chooses to be paralyzed by fear. The behavior that frustrates you is usually a symptom of a system trying to protect itself from a perceived threat. Once you realize that they are suffering just as much as you are frustrated, the anger begins to lose its edge.

4. The Loved One's Emotional Cycle

When you love someone with anxiety, you do not just watch them struggle. You go through a profound, exhausting emotional cycle of your own. This cycle dictates almost every interaction in your home.

Confusion: It starts here. You do not understand why they are stuck. You question the seriousness of the problem and assume they just need a little push or a better schedule.

Fix-It Mode: When the push does not work, you take over. You want things to run smoothly, so you do the laundry, make the phone calls, and manage the calendar. You think, If I just clear their plate, they will feel better.

Frustration: The tasks keep piling up, and the freeze continues. You realize that clearing their plate did not fix the anxiety; it just gave you more work.

Resentment: You start keeping a mental scorecard. You feel like a martyr carrying the entire weight of the household, and you resent them for not carrying their share. You begin to snap over small things.

Fear: Late at night, when the anger cools, you look at the life you are building together and wonder, Is this just how things are going to be forever?

Guilt: You feel terrible for being angry at someone who is clearly suffering. You tell yourself you need to be a better, more patient partner.

Trying Again: Fueled by guilt, you wake up the next morning determined to be supportive, resetting the cycle back to Confusion.

You cannot stop this emotional cycle from happening. It is a natural human response to prolonged stress. But you can recognize it. You can stop weaponizing your frustration during the resentment phase. You can learn to step away when you are angry, rather than delivering that anger to a person whose nervous system is already overloaded.

5. Reader Reflection Exercise

Before we move forward, take ten minutes to answer these questions honestly. You do not have to share these answers with anyone, but you need to see them for yourself.

What is the most common assumption I make when my loved one avoids a task?

When was the last time I mistook a nervous system freeze for intentional laziness?

What specific behavior (unopened mail, canceled plans, messy rooms) triggers my frustration the fastest?

Why do I take that specific behavior personally?

How often do I jump into "Fix-It Mode" instead of just sitting with them?

When I feel resentment building, how does my tone of voice change when I speak to them?

What am I most afraid of when I look at their current struggle?

Have I been demanding that they experience the world the same way I do?

Can I accept that their inconsistency is a symptom of anxiety, rather than a lack of effort?

What is one way I can pause this week before reacting to their avoidance?

6. What to Practice This Week

Changing how you view anxiety is not a mental switch you flip once; it is a habit you build over time. To start retraining your perspective, we are going to break this down into a daily practice plan.

-Monday: Notice one assumption.
When you feel a spike of frustration because they left a dish on the counter or ignored an email, catch the assumption your brain makes ("They are so lazy"). Name it silently to yourself, and then actively remind yourself: They are overloaded, not lazy. Just notice the thought today. Do not try to fix anything else.

-Tuesday: Ask one curiosity-based question.
Instead of giving a command or offering a solution, ask a question designed purely to understand their experience. Try: "What does that task feel like to you right now?" or "Is your brain running really fast today?" Listen to the answer without correcting it.

-Wednesday: Practice the five-minute pause.
When they cancel plans or withdraw into silence, force yourself to wait five minutes before reacting. Use that

time to remember the Common Misreads. Remind yourself that the outside behavior is protecting a highly vulnerable internal state. Let the initial wave of your own frustration pass before you speak.

-Thursday: Offer low-pressure support.
Find one small task they are avoiding, like opening the mail or choosing dinner. Offer a bridge. Say, "I know this feels heavy today. Can I just sit with you while you do it, or can I handle the first step for you?"

-Friday: Reflect on the emotional cycle.
Look back at the week. Where were you in the Loved One's Emotional Cycle? Did you jump into Fix-It Mode? Did you feel resentment building? Acknowledge where you are without judging yourself. Awareness is the first step to breaking the cycle.

You have to let go of the idea that their anxiety is about you. It is not a reflection of your worth, and their inability to complete a task is not a sign of disrespect.

Now that you understand what the freeze looks like from the outside, and how easy it is to misread it, the next step is understanding exactly what it feels like from the inside. We need to look at the mechanics of the anxious brain, so you can stop arguing with it and start supporting it.

Chapter 2: What Anxiety Can Feel Like From the Inside

1. The Reality of the Body Alarm

In the last chapter, we looked at how anxiety behaves from the outside. We talked about how easy it is to misread a frozen nervous system as laziness, manipulation, or a lack of care.

Now, we need to go inside. We need to look at what your loved one is actually experiencing when they are staring blankly at the kitchen sink or avoiding a simple phone call.

Before we start, you need to understand one crucial rule: This will not make logical sense at first.

If you try to understand their experience using your own logical, step-by-step thinking, you will only end up frustrated again. Anxiety is not a logical process. It is a biological alarm system responding to a false positive. The danger they are reacting to may not be real, but the fear they are feeling in their body is completely real.

2. Deep Dive: The Body Alarm

Anxiety is not just a series of worried thoughts. It is a profound physical event. When the brain perceives a threat, even if that threat is just a pile of laundry or an unopened envelope, it dumps adrenaline and cortisol into the bloodstream.

This is the "body alarm."

Within seconds, their heart rate spikes. Their breathing becomes shallow, depriving their brain of the oxygen it needs to think clearly. Their chest tightens. Their face flushes with heat. Their muscles tense up, preparing to either fight a predator or run for their life. Their stomach might drop, and their legs might feel entirely frozen to the floor.

This adrenaline cycle is incredibly taxing. The body is running at maximum capacity, preparing for a physical battle that never actually happens. When the alarm finally passes, the adrenaline crash leaves them physically and mentally exhausted, even if they have done nothing visible all day.

They are tired from fighting something you cannot see.

When the body alarm sounds, the logical part of the brain shuts down. They are no longer thinking about how to complete a chore; they are experiencing an overwhelming, primal urgency to escape.

3. Five Scenarios: The Internal Spirals

To understand why a simple task can become impossible, you have to understand the speed and the weight of the thoughts that come with the body alarm. The disconnect between their past capability and their current paralysis is where frustration begins. Let us look at five common scenarios to see how this disconnect plays out inside their mind and body.

Scenario 1: The Dishwashing Thought Spiral

Imagine your loved one walking into the kitchen. They see a sink full of dishes. To a non-anxious brain, the thought process is linear: There are dishes. I should wash them. I will turn on the water.

But inside the anxious brain, the sight of the dishes triggers an immediate, catastrophic chain reaction. The thought process looks like this:

There are dishes. I need to wash them. The water needs to be hot. What if the water is too hot and I drop that slippery glass plate? If I drop the plate, it will shatter. If it shatters, a piece will definitely cut my foot. If I cut my foot, I won't be able to put my work shoes on tomorrow. If I can't wear my shoes, I can't go to work. If I miss work again, my boss is going to fire me. If I get fired, we won't be able to pay the mortgage. If we can't pay the mortgage, we are going to lose the house. We are going to go bankrupt, and it will be entirely my fault because I tried to wash a glass plate.

By the time they reach the sponge, their chest is tight, their breathing is shallow, and they are trying to prevent a financial disaster that has not happened.

What you see: They are standing in front of the sink, doing nothing.

What may be happening: Their brain has turned the dishes into a life-or-death threat, and their body is frozen in terror. They are experiencing a physical body alarm over a glass plate.

Mishandled response: "Just wash the dishes. It takes five minutes." (This dismisses the invisible bear they are currently fighting.)

Handled-well response: "Hey, I can see you're stuck. I am going to wash the glass plates, and you can just do the silverware if you want."

Why this works: It breaks the catastrophic chain. By removing the specific item that triggered the spiral (the glass plate), you remove the perceived threat and lower the body alarm.

Scenario 2: The Phone Call Thought Chain

This same rapid-fire catastrophizing applies to almost every task that requires interaction with the outside world. Phone calls are notoriously difficult because of the uncontrollable variables on the other end of the line.

Suppose your loved one needs to call the mechanic to ask a simple question about a repair estimate. They pick up the phone, and the chain begins:

I need to call the mechanic. What if he answers and I forget the name of the part? If I forget the name, he's going to think I'm an idiot. He's going to talk down to me. What if he tells me the repair is actually three times more expensive than the estimate? I won't know how to argue with him. I'll just agree to it because I'll panic. If I agree to it, we won't have enough money for groceries this week. I'll have ruined the budget because I'm too weak to stand up for myself on the phone.

Their palms are sweating. Their throat is tight. Before the phone even rings, they are already grieving the loss of their grocery budget and their self-respect.

What you see: The mechanic's number has been sitting on the counter for two days.

What may be happening: They are paralyzed by the fear of humiliation and financial ruin. The phone feels like it weighs a hundred pounds, and their body is reacting as if they are about to be attacked.

Mishandled response: "Why haven't you called them yet? You are being completely irresponsible." (This confirms their fear that they are weak and failing.)

Handled-well response: "I know phone calls are heavy right now. Do you want me to sit with you while you call, or do you want to write down exactly what you want to say before you dial?"

Why this works: It offers a safety net without immediately taking the task away from them. Writing down a script reduces the fear of forgetting the part name, and your steady presence gives them backup if the body alarm gets too loud.

Scenario 3: The Unopened Mail

The internal speed of anxiety attaches itself to anything that represents an external demand. When an anxious person looks at a stack of unopened mail, they do not see paper. They see a stack of demands, bad news, and potential failures.

There's a letter from the IRS. What if we owe them thousands of dollars? What if it's an audit? If we get audited, they will find out I made a mistake on our taxes three years ago. I'll go to jail. Or there's a medical bill. What if insurance didn't cover that test? What if it's a collections notice? If it's collections, our credit score will tank, and we'll never be able to move.

The fear is so intense that the safest option is simply not to open the mail. If the envelope stays sealed, the catastrophe remains a possibility, not a reality.

What you see: They are ignoring the mail and letting it pile up on the counter.

What may be happening: They are terrified of what the mail will confirm about their life. Their heart races every time they walk past the pile.

Mishandled response: "You are acting like a child. Just open the envelopes." (This adds shame to the terror.)

Handled-well response: "Let's open these together. I will open them, and I will tell you what they are before you have to look at them."

Why this works: You become a buffer between them and the perceived threat. By previewing the contents, you remove the element of surprise, which is the primary fuel for the body alarm.

<u>Scenario 4:</u> The Grocery Store

To understand how this physical alarm dictates behavior in public, let us look at a common environment that frequently triggers a massive internal response: the grocery store.

You are walking down the cereal aisle. The grocery store is a sensory nightmare for an overloaded nervous system. The bright fluorescent lights, the overlapping music and announcements, the crowded aisles, and the sheer volume of choices create intense decision fatigue. Their brain is trying to process fifty different stimuli at once.

The body alarm triggers. Their chest tightens, and they feel a sudden, terrifying wave of panic. They are convinced they are going to pass out or lose control in public. Leaving the store is not a choice; it is a desperate bid for physical safety. They abandon the half-full cart and walk briskly toward the exit.

What you see: They suddenly abandon the cart and walk out of the store, leaving you confused and annoyed.

What may be happening: They have hit absolute sensory overload. Their body is in full flight mode, and they are escaping to prevent a public breakdown.

Mishandled response: "Are you kidding me? We just got here. You can't just leave the cart in the middle of the aisle. Just push through it for ten more minutes." (This forces them to stay in an environment their body is registering as a severe threat, escalating the panic.)

Handled-well response: "Okay, let's go. I'll leave the cart here. We can figure out dinner later."

Why this works: This validates their need for safety and removes the pressure immediately. You are not arguing with the body alarm; you are helping them escape the trigger.

Scenario 5: The Email / Work Task

The body alarm does not just trigger in crowded places. It frequently triggers in total silence, sitting in front of a computer screen.

They have to send a three-sentence email to their boss summarizing a project. Perfectionism and anxiety are deeply intertwined. The thought of sending the email triggers an intense fear of being judged, misunderstood, or exposed as incompetent. The brain begins a catastrophic delay loop:

If I use the wrong tone, my boss will think I am disrespectful. If I leave out a detail, they will think I am sloppy. I need to make it perfect.

The pressure to be flawless causes the body alarm to spike. They type and delete the email four times.

Finally, they open a new tab and start scrolling through social media.

What you see: They are scrolling instead of answering an email.

What may be happening: They are numbing a body alarm while perfectionism makes the email feel dangerous. The scrolling is a desperate attempt to lower the volume of the internal noise.

Mishandled response: "Why is it taking you two hours to write three sentences? Just hit send. You are overthinking this." (This dismisses the intense fear they are experiencing and adds shame to the paralysis.)

Handled-well response: "Emails can feel so heavy sometimes. Do you want me to read it over for you, or do you want to step away for a bit and try again later?"

Why this works: This normalizes the difficulty and offers practical, low-pressure support. It tells them that they are not crazy for finding a simple task impossible today.

4. What You Miss in Real Time

Because the body alarm is internal, what you see on the outside is often the exact opposite of what is happening on the inside. You are looking at their coping mechanisms, not their panic. To support them effectively, you have to learn to translate what you see into what they are actually feeling.

What you see: They go completely silent in the middle of a conversation.

What may be happening: They are experiencing sensory overload. Their brain cannot process one more piece of auditory input, including your voice. The silence is a protective mechanism.

Better translation: "This is not stubbornness. This is a system shutdown."

What you see: They are scrolling mindlessly on their phone while chores pile up.

What may be happening: The internal noise is so loud and terrifying that they are using the rapid dopamine hits of a screen to force their brain to focus on something else. They are numbing the body alarm.

Better translation: "This is not laziness. This is a desperate distraction technique."

What you see: They are lying down in the middle of the day.

What may be happening: The adrenaline crash has hit, and their body physically cannot remain upright or engaged. They are recovering from an invisible marathon.

Better translation: "They are not giving up. They are physically exhausted from fighting their own nervous system."

5. Why They Can Do It Sometimes

This is perhaps the most frustrating aspect for a loved one: the inconsistency. Yesterday, they went to the grocery store, cooked dinner, and laughed with friends. Today, they cannot get off the couch to take a shower.

This inconsistency often leads loved ones to a very dangerous conclusion: If they could do it yesterday, they can do it today. They are just choosing when to try.

You have to challenge this thought every time it appears. A good day does not mean they have suddenly gained control over their anxiety. It simply means their capacity was higher that day.

Capacity fluctuates wildly based on factors you cannot see: how well they slept, the cumulative stress of the week, hormonal shifts, or subconscious triggers. On a good day, the body alarm is quiet, and their executive function is online. On a hard day, the alarm is blaring, and the system is offline.

Inconsistency is not a choice. It is the defining feature of a fluctuating nervous system. When you demand that they perform at their "good day" level every day, you are demanding the impossible.

6. Why Logic Does Not Work Here

When you see your loved one frozen over an email or fleeing a grocery store, your instinct is usually to point out the logic. You want to remind them that the email is only three sentences, or that the store is perfectly safe. You think that if you just explain the facts clearly enough, the anxiety will break.

This never works.

It does not work because the anxious brain is reacting as if the danger is happening right now. When the body alarm is sounding, the logical part of the brain is offline. You cannot logic someone out of a biological response.

If a bear is chasing you, and someone runs up beside you and says, "Actually, statistically speaking, bear attacks are very rare," you are not going to stop running. The facts might be true, but they do not immediately calm the body.

When you say, "Just send the email, it's not a big deal," you are completely dismissing the invisible bear they are currently fighting. Your logical request feels incredibly jarring because it does not match the intensity of the fear they are experiencing in their body. It makes them feel crazy, unsupported, and deeply misunderstood.

7. Reader Reflection Exercise

Take a moment to sit with what you have just read. The goal here is not to make you feel guilty for misunderstanding their anxiety; the goal is to help you see it clearly so you can respond differently. Answer these questions honestly for yourself:

When do I assume they have control over their behavior, when they are actually just out of capacity?

Do I treat their good days as proof that they "could do it if they really wanted to"?

When they shut down or go silent, how quickly do I take it personally?

Have I ever told them they were overreacting to something that felt physically terrifying to them?

How often do I try to use logic to talk them out of a panic response?

When I see them scrolling on their phone during a stressful moment, what is my immediate assumption?

Can I recognize the difference between intentional laziness and a nervous system freeze?

How does it change my perspective to know they are physically exhausted from fighting an invisible alarm?

What is the hardest part for me about accepting their fluctuating capacity?

What is one specific situation where I need to stop pushing and start observing?

8. What to Practice This Week

Understanding the internal experience of anxiety requires practice. You are learning a new language. This week, focus on this daily practice plan:

-Monday: Observe without correcting.
When you see them avoiding a task or shutting down, do not intervene immediately. Do not offer a solution, and do not point out the logic. Just watch them, and remind yourself: Their body alarm is going off right now.

-Tuesday: Name the body alarm.
Stop using words like "lazy," "stubborn," or "dramatic" in your own mind. When they leave a room abruptly, label it neutrally: They reached their sensory limit. When they cannot make a phone call, label it neutrally: They are stuck in a thought spiral.

-Wednesday: Stop using logic as a first response.
When they express a fear about a task, do not immediately tell them why they are wrong. Do not offer statistics or facts. Instead, validate the feeling first. Say, "That sounds really overwhelming," before you say anything else.

-Thursday: Reduce pressure for one task.
Find one specific task they are struggling with today. It could be making dinner, answering an email, or doing laundry. Remove the expectation entirely. Tell them, "Do not worry about the laundry today. We will figure it out tomorrow." Notice how their body responds to the removed pressure.

-Friday: Reflect on capacity versus control.
Look back at the week. Did they have a good day followed by a hard day? Remind yourself that the hard

day is not a choice. They did not lose control; their capacity simply dropped.

Once you understand how real the danger feels inside their body, it becomes much easier to see why applying blunt force and pressure always backfires. When you push someone who is already terrified, you do not motivate them. You just make them more afraid. In the next chapter, we will look exactly at how pressure breaks trust, and how to offer support without accidentally feeding the panic.

Chapter 3: Why Pressure Usually Backfires

1. The Instinct to Push

You are trying to help. You are doing exactly what should work. You are offering solutions, setting reasonable expectations, and trying to motivate your loved one to break out of their anxiety freeze.

And yet, you are getting worse results.

The harder you push, the deeper they retreat. The more you try to help them organize their life, the more helpless they seem to become. You are likely feeling confused, deeply frustrated, and perhaps slightly desperate. You are watching someone you love struggle with something that looks small from the outside, and every time you reach out to help, the situation seems to get heavier.

The problem is not that you do not care. The problem is not that they are refusing to try.

The problem is that your natural instincts are working against you.

When you see someone stuck, your instinct is to apply pressure to get them moving. But to a nervous system that is already overwhelmed by a perceived threat, pressure does not feel like motivation. Pressure feels like an attack. In this chapter, we are going to look at the three most common ways loved ones accidentally apply pressure, why those instincts backfire, and what you must do instead.

2. The Three Types of Accidental Pressure

The Logic Mismatch

Because you are not trapped in an anxiety spiral, your brain defaults to the most effective tool it has: logic. Logical people rely on logic because it works in almost every other area of life. You assume that if you just explain why the task is easy, or why the fear is unfounded, the anxiety will evaporate.

What you are trying to do:
You are trying to be a reasonable coach. You want to show them that the mountain they are staring at is actually just a small hill. You believe that facts will set them free.

What the anxious person experiences:
They may hear that their fear is unreasonable, inconvenient, or stupid. When you use logic to point out how simple the task is, you are unintentionally proving to them how broken they are. The message they hear is: This is incredibly easy, and the fact that you cannot do it means you are failing at basic adulthood.

Why it backfires:
There is a fundamental mismatch with their body state. You cannot use a math problem to turn off a fire alarm. Logic demands that they use the prefrontal cortex, which is currently offline due to the body

alarm. It causes a massive shame spike, leading to immediate shutdown.

Better response:
Validate the physical difficulty before you ever discuss the facts of the task. Say, "I know this feels impossible right now," instead of "This should be easy."

The Urgency Trap

If logic is your first instinct, urgency is usually your second. When logic fails, frustration builds. You start to feel like you are carrying the entire weight of the household, and you need them to pull their weight now. You start using deadlines, consequences, and a raised voice to try and shock them into action.

What you are trying to do:
You are trying to force compliance to keep the household running. You want to break through their freeze by creating a deadline that they cannot ignore.

What the anxious person experiences:
Time pressure equals threat amplification. When you say, "We need to leave now," or "You have to do this right now," you are sending a massive danger signal to a brain that is already terrified. Your tone and your speed matter just as much as your words. They feel cornered and attacked.

Why it backfires:
It increases the perceived threat. Urgency might get the immediate task done through sheer panic, but it makes the next task significantly harder because it

damages trust. It makes it much more likely that they will associate you with fear rather than safety.

Better response:
Remove the artificial timeline. Say, "This needs to get done tonight, but it does not have to be right this second. Take twenty minutes to decompress first."

The Fix-It Energy

The most insidious form of pressure does not look like anger or logic. It looks like extreme helpfulness. It is the "fix-it" energy. When you love someone who is suffering, your deepest desire is to remove their pain. So, when they hit a wall, you jump into project-manager mode. You start firing off solutions, making lists, and trying to organize their life so the anxiety cannot touch them.

What you are trying to do:
You are trying to be the perfect partner. You want to rescue them from the overwhelming task by doing the heavy lifting yourself.

What the anxious person experiences:
They can feel entirely incapable. When you solve it for them, their brain learns that they cannot solve it themselves. You are accidentally sending the message: You cannot handle this, so I have to.

Why it backfires:
It reinforces learned helplessness and strips away their agency. The anxiety might temporarily recede because you took over the scary task, but it is immediately

replaced by a deep, hollow shame. They emotionally check out of the process entirely and may become even more dependent on you.

Better response:
Offer a bridge, not a rescue. Say, "Do you want me to do this with you, or do you want to try the first step while I sit here?"

3. Three Scenarios: Pressure in Practice

<u>Scenario 1:</u> The Saturday Cleaning Push

What you see: It is Saturday morning. The living room is a mess, and your loved one has been sitting on the couch staring at their phone for two hours.

What you are trying to do: You are using logic to motivate them. You want to show them how quickly the problem can be solved so you can both enjoy the weekend.

What they hear: "You are lazy, and you are ruining our Saturday over twenty minutes of easy work."

Mishandled response: "If we just spend twenty minutes picking up right now, it will be done. It is really not that much stuff. Just grab the trash. It is easy." (This turns "easy" into a weapon that induces shame.)

Handled-well response: "Saturday mornings are always harder than they feel like they should be, aren't they? I am going to start on the kitchen. If you want to grab the trash later, that would be great."

Why this works: It removes the logic and the timeline. It validates that starting is hard, and it offers an invitation to participate without a demand for immediate compliance.

Scenario 2: The Leaving-the-House Deadline

What you see: You are supposed to leave for a family event in ten minutes. Your loved one is pacing the hallway, changing their shirt for the third time, and breathing heavily.

What you are trying to do: You are using urgency to keep them on schedule. You do not want to be late, and you want to snap them out of their pacing loop.

What they hear: "You are an embarrassment, and you are about to ruin this event for everyone."

Mishandled response: "We have to leave right now. Stop changing your clothes. We are going to be late, and everyone is waiting for us. Just get in the car." (This time pressure acts like gasoline on the fire of their panic.)

Handled-well response: "Hey, look at me. We do not have to rush. I will text them and say we are running fifteen minutes behind. Take your time."

Why this works: It immediately lowers the threat level. By removing the strict deadline, you give their nervous system room to breathe. The irony is that removing the urgency often helps them get out the door faster than yelling does.

Scenario 3: The Paperwork Takeover

What you see: They are sitting at the dining table, surrounded by scattered medical bills, completely frozen and quietly crying.

What you are trying to do: You are using fix-it energy to rescue them from the overwhelming administrative nightmare.

What they hear: "You are too fragile to handle adult responsibilities, so I will treat you like a child and do it for you."

Mishandled response: "Okay, stop crying, let's just knock this out. Give me the pile. I will make a spreadsheet, I will call the insurance company tomorrow, and I will just handle all of it. You don't have to worry about it." (This creates immediate relief followed by crushing long-term shame and loss of agency.)

Handled-well response: "This looks incredibly overwhelming. What if we just find the one bill that is due soonest, put a sticky note on it, and put the rest away in a folder for today?"

Why this works: It breaks the task down into a manageable piece without taking the steering wheel out of their hands. It preserves their agency while offering highly specific, limited support.

4. Same Words, Different Pressure

It is crucial to understand that pressure is not just about the words you choose. You can use the exact right script, but if your delivery is wrong, the anxious brain will still register it as an attack. Even helpful words can become intense pressure if:

Your tone is sharp or clipped.

Your timing is bad (interrupting them when they are already visibly overwhelmed).

Your body language is tense (crossed arms, sighing heavily, rolling your eyes).

You are standing over them while they are sitting down.

For example, the phrase, "I am just trying to help," is objectively kind. But if you say it loudly, with a sharp tone, while standing over them as they struggle to send an email, it lands as an accusation. It translates to: I am being a good partner, and you are being difficult and ungrateful.

The anxious brain is hyper-vigilant. It scans your face, your posture, and your tone for signs of danger. If your body is radiating frustration, your perfectly crafted words will not matter.

5. Common Pressure Phrases

We all have default phrases we use when we are frustrated. Here are some of the most common pressure phrases, what your loved one actually hears, and what you should try instead.

Pressure phrase:
"Just do it."

What they may hear:
"You are failing at something basic and making this harder than it has to be."

Try instead:
"Let's make this smaller. What is the very first step?"

Pressure phrase:
"You are overthinking this."

What they may hear:
"Your reality is stupid and your feelings are invalid."

Try instead:
"Your brain is running really fast right now. Let's take a break."

Pressure phrase:
"We don't have time for this."

What they may hear:
"You are a burden and an inconvenience to my schedule."

Try instead:
"There is no rush. We can adjust the plan."

Pressure phrase:
"Why are you making this such a big deal?"

What they may hear:
"You are being dramatic, and your fear does not make sense."

Try instead:
"I can see how heavy this feels for you today."

Pressure phrase:
"I will just do it myself."

What they may hear:
"You are useless, and I resent you."

Try instead:
"Do you want to tackle this together later?"

Pressure phrase:
"You just need to calm down."

What they may hear:
"I cannot handle your emotions, and you need to hide them from me."

Try instead:
"I am right here with you. Take your time."

6. What Pressure Costs

When you rely on logic, urgency, or fix-it energy, you might occasionally force your loved one through a task. They might take out the trash or get in the car. But that short-term victory comes at a devastating long-term cost.

Every time you apply pressure to a frozen nervous system, you trigger a massive shame spike. They feel broken for needing to be pushed. This shame leads directly to a deeper shutdown.

Worse, it causes a profound loss of trust. If you are the person who applies pressure when they are terrified, you are no longer a safe harbor; you become part of the threat. They will begin to hide their struggles from you to avoid your logic or your urgency.

Over time, constant pressure creates learned helplessness. They will stop trying to initiate tasks at all, waiting for you to either yell at them or do it for them. By pushing them to act today, you are making more avoidance tomorrow much more likely.

7. Reader Reflection Exercise

Before we move to the daily practice, take a few minutes to answer these questions honestly. The goal is to recognize your own default habits.

When my loved one is stuck, do I usually reach for logic, urgency, or fix-it energy first?

What specific tone of voice do I use when I am trying to "motivate" them out of frustration?

Do I try to create artificial deadlines or urgency to force them into action?

When was the last time I took over a task completely instead of supporting them through it?

Which of the "Common Pressure Phrases" do I use the most often?

How does my body language change when I am waiting for them to finish something?

Have I ever told them a task was "easy" while they were clearly panicking over it?

Do I view their anxiety as a problem I need to solve as quickly as possible?

Can I see how my attempts to help might actually be making them feel more isolated?

What is one specific way I can lower the pressure in our home tomorrow?

8. What to Practice This Week

To break the habit of applying pressure, you need a structured plan. Follow these steps this week to start changing your default responses.

-Monday: Notice your pressure instinct.
Today, do not try to change anything. Just watch

yourself. Notice when you feel the urge to use logic, create a deadline, or take over a task. Silently name the instinct to yourself: I am trying to use fix-it energy right now.

-Tuesday: Slow your tone.
Focus entirely on your voice today. When you speak to them about a task, a chore, or a plan, consciously lower your volume and slow your speaking speed by ten percent. Notice how a calmer tone changes the energy in the room.

-Wednesday: Replace one logic statement.
When you catch yourself about to explain why a task is easy or why a fear is illogical, stop. Replace the logic with validation. Say, "I know this is really hard right now," and leave it at that.

-Thursday: Ask before helping.
Resist the fix-it energy. Before you jump in to organize their paperwork or make a phone call for them, ask a bridge question: "Do you want me to do this with you, or do you want to try the first step while I sit here?"

-Friday: Stop one task from escalating.
When you feel the urgency building—when you are about to say, "We have to leave right now" or "Just do it"—force yourself to remove the deadline. Tell them, "Take your time, there is no rush," even if it means you are five minutes late.

You are not a bad person for wanting to push them forward. You just need to recognize that the push is hurting them. Once you stop applying pressure, you create the space for them to actually start moving. In the next chapter, we will look at how to safely rebuild their momentum using the exact opposite of pressure.

Chapter 4: Small Wins Change the Game

1. The Progress Mismatch

In the last chapter, we looked at why pressure backfires. We saw how pushing an anxious person to move faster or do more only increases their paralysis.

Now, we need to talk about what actually works. But before we can do that, we have to address a fundamental mismatch in how you and your loved one measure progress.

When you look at your life together, you want big changes. You want consistency. You want visible progress: a clean house, a completed to-do list, a return to normalcy.

But when your loved one is trapped inside a body alarm, they cannot give you big changes. They can only manage tiny steps. Their effort is wildly inconsistent. And most of their wins are entirely invisible to you.

You are looking for progress you can see. They are fighting battles you cannot.

This mismatch is the source of endless heartbreak. When you measure their day by what is left undone on the kitchen counter, you look at them and think, Nothing is happening. They are not even trying.

But the reality is that they are exerting constant, exhausting internal effort just to survive the day. Effort does not always equal visible output. Surviving a panic attack is not laziness. If you do not change how you measure progress, you will continually erase their hardest work, and nothing else in this book will help. Small wins are not cute. They are the foundation of rebuilding capacity.

2. Five Scenarios: The Reality of Small Wins

To support someone with anxiety, you have to completely redefine what a "win" looks like. Progress is not big. Progress is not fast. Progress is small, repeatable, and safe. To a non-anxious person, these things feel "too small" to count. They feel like the bare minimum requirements of being alive. But when anxiety is draining all available energy, doing the basics requires massive effort. Let us look at five scenarios to understand what these wins actually look like.

<u>Scenario 1:</u> Getting Water

What you see: They finally get out of bed at 1:00 PM, walk into the kitchen, and pour a glass of water.

Why it looks too small: Drinking water is a basic human function. It takes thirty seconds and requires no special skill.

What it actually required: It required a three-hour internal fight with their own shame before they finally found the courage to put their feet on the floor. It required pushing past the physical weight of the adrenaline crash just to stand upright.

Mishandled response: "Finally up. Can you please start the laundry now?" (This ignores the massive internal hurdle they just cleared and immediately raises expectations.)

Handled-well response: "Hey. Glad you are up. Take your time today."

Why this works: You name the effort and protect their energy. Their nervous system calms down because they feel safe, not evaluated.

<u>Scenario 2:</u> Eating Toast

What you see: They have not eaten a real meal in two days. They finally make a single piece of dry toast and eat half of it.

Why it looks too small: It is not a balanced meal. It does not solve the larger problem of their physical health or their disrupted routine.

What it actually required: Anxiety kills the appetite. Their stomach is tied in knots, and the thought of chewing and swallowing feels physically repulsive. Eating that toast required them to override a profound physical aversion to food.

Mishandled response: "Is that all you are going to eat? You need protein. You are going to make yourself sick." (This turns a victory over nausea into a lecture about nutrition.)

Handled-well response: "I am really glad you got something to eat. Do you want me to leave the bread out in case you want more later?"

Why this works: It validates the action without demanding more. It leaves the door open for further progress without applying pressure.

<u>Scenario 3:</u> Answering One Text

What you see: They have been ignoring their phone for three days. They finally pick it up, type a four-word reply to a friend, and put the phone face down again.

Why it looks too small: They still have twenty unread messages. Answering one text does not fix their social isolation or clear their inbox.

What it actually required: It required massive emotional exposure. It required them to risk engaging with the outside world while their heart was racing, pushing past the fear that they are a bad friend.

Mishandled response: "Good, you finally texted Sarah back. Now you need to reply to your mom." (This treats the first text as a stepping stone to more work, rather than a standalone victory.)

Handled-well response: "I know looking at your phone is really hard right now. Good job answering Sarah."

Why this works: It acknowledges the specific fear attached to the phone and celebrates the courage it took to engage with it, even for ten seconds.

Scenario 4: Opening One Envelope

What you see: There is a stack of mail on the counter. They open one envelope, glance at the bill inside, and walk away from the pile.

Why it looks too small: The pile is still there. The bill is not paid. The administrative problem has not been solved.

What it actually required: It required them to face a tangible piece of paper that their brain was registering as a life-or-death threat. It required them to willingly trigger their own body alarm and survive the spike in panic.

Mishandled response: "You opened one? Are you just going to leave the rest of them sitting there?" (This punishes them for stopping before the entire task is complete.)

Handled-well response: "That was a really brave step. We can look at the rest of them tomorrow."

Why this works: It recognizes the bravery required to face a trigger and immediately removes the pressure to continue.

Scenario 5: Turning on the Laptop

What you see: They have been avoiding work all week. They sit down at the desk, open the laptop, stare at the screen for two minutes, and close it again.

Why it looks too small: They did not actually do any work. No emails were sent, and no projects were advanced.

What it actually required: It required them to willingly sit in the exact location where their perfectionism and fear of failure are most intense. They exposed themselves to the trigger, even if they could not yet execute a task.

Mishandled response: "You didn't even do anything. Why did you even bother opening it?" (This completely invalidates the exposure therapy they just attempted.)

Handled-well response: "Sitting at the desk is the hardest part. You did good today. Let's try again tomorrow."

Why this works: It separates the act of showing up from the expectation of productivity. It makes the desk a slightly safer place for tomorrow.

3. How Loved Ones Erase Wins

Even when you start to notice these small wins, your default language can accidentally erase them. When you minimize a win, their brain immediately learns a devastating lesson: Nothing I do counts unless it fixes the entire problem. Their motivation drops to zero. The shame returns. The avoidance increases. Here are the common ways loved ones erase wins, and what to say instead.

What you say: "Since you're up, can you..."

What they hear: "Your energy does not belong to you. The moment you have any, I will spend it for you."

Better replacement phrase: "I am glad you are up. Let me know if you need anything."

What you say: "That's all?"

What they hear: "Your hardest effort is still pathetic and insufficient."

Better replacement phrase: "That counts. That is enough for right now."

What you say: "Good, now do the next thing."

What they hear: "You are not allowed to rest until the entire list is finished."

Better replacement phrase: "Great job getting that done. Let's take a break."

What you say: "Finally."

What they hear: "I have been silently judging and resenting you this entire time."

Better replacement phrase: "I know that took a lot out of you. I am proud of you."

4. The Invisible Effort

You have to learn to see the effort that does not look like progress. When you measure their day by what is left undone, you are missing the profound work they are doing internally.

Resisting panic: When they are sitting quietly on the couch while the house is chaotic, you might see avoidance. What you do not see is them actively resisting the urge to run away, actively trying to regulate their breathing, and actively choosing to stay in the room with you.

Staying in the room: When they go silent during a difficult conversation, you might see stubbornness. What you do not see is them fighting the overwhelming biological urge to flee the house to escape the sensory overload.

Choosing not to spiral: When they stare blankly out the window for twenty minutes, you might see dissociation. What you do not see is them aggressively interrupting a catastrophic thought chain about financial ruin before it takes root.

Asking for help: When they finally admit they cannot make a phone call, you might see weakness. What you do not see is the massive blow to their ego they just accepted in order to communicate their limits to you honestly.

Stopping before collapse: When they abandon a chore halfway through, you might see laziness. What you do not see is them recognizing their own nervous system limits and choosing to stop before they trigger a multi-day crash.

5. Stop on a High Note

Once you start looking for small wins, you will inevitably encounter a "Good Day." A Good Day is when the anxiety lifts, the energy returns, and they suddenly want to clean the garage, do the taxes, and run five errands.

As a loved one, you will be thrilled. You will want to ride this wave of productivity as long as possible. You will think, Finally, we are getting caught up.

Do not do this. Good days are incredibly fragile and highly dangerous.

When an anxious person feels good, they often try to overcompensate for all the days they felt bad. They feel guilty for their previous lack of capacity, so they overdo it. They push their nervous system past its actual limit.

More is not always better. The inevitable result of a massive productivity binge is a massive, days-long crash. That crash triggers a brutal shame loop: I am broken again. I will never get better.

You have to help them stop on a high note.

If they have run two errands and suggest a third, you have to step in. Say, "You have gotten so much done today. Let's stop here so you have energy left for tomorrow."

Stopping early feels wrong. It feels counterintuitive to halt progress when they are finally moving. But stopping early protects tomorrow. It teaches their nervous system that it is allowed to rest before it collapses. It proves that their worth is not tied to how much they can produce in a single manic burst.

6. Reader Reflection Exercise

Take a few minutes to evaluate how you have been measuring progress in your home. Answer these questions honestly:

1. Do I measure my loved one's progress by what they accomplished, or by what is left undone?

2. Have I ever used the phrase "Since you're up, can you..." to assign a chore?

3. When they complete a small task, do I immediately suggest the next one?

4. How often do I recognize the invisible effort of them simply staying in the room during a hard moment?

5. Have I ever rolled my eyes or sighed when they only finished half of a task?

6. Do I secretly believe that if they can do one small thing, they should be able to do a big thing?

7. When they have a "Good Day," do I push them to keep going until they are exhausted?

8. How hard is it for me to accept that drinking a glass of water might be their biggest win of the day?

9. Do I understand that surviving a panic attack requires as much energy as running a race?

10. What is one small win I completely ignored or minimized this week?

7. What to Practice This Week

Changing how you measure progress is a fundamental shift in perspective. Use this five-day plan to practice seeing and protecting the small wins.

-Monday: Notice one small win. Do not say anything out loud today. Just watch them. Find one tiny action—eating a piece of toast, opening a piece of mail, or just getting off the couch—and silently acknowledge the massive effort it required.

-Tuesday: Say it out loud. When you see a small win today, name it. Say, "I know looking at your phone is hard right now. Good job answering that text." Do not add a follow-up request. Just name the win and walk away.

-Wednesday: Do not add another task. When they complete a chore or a task today, absolutely forbid yourself from suggesting the next step. If they wash one dish, do not ask them to wipe the counters. Let the single win stand alone.

-Thursday: Celebrate without patronizing. Acknowledge a win using a tone of genuine respect, not the tone you would use for a toddler. Say, "That took a lot more effort than it looks like. I am proud of you."

-Friday: Help them stop on a high note. When you see them gaining momentum and starting a second or third task, gently intervene. Tell them, "You have done enough for today. Let's stop here so you are not exhausted tomorrow." Protect their energy for them.

You are not trying to get them back to who they were. You are helping them rebuild capacity safely. When you learn to see the invisible effort, when you protect the small wins, and when you enforce stopping on a high note, you create an environment where healing is actually possible.

In the next chapter, we are going to introduce the tool that makes this possible. We are going to look at how to take these small, invisible wins and turn them into undeniable proof of life.

Chapter 5: What Helpful Support Actually Sounds Like

1. The Language of Safety

By now, you understand why pressure backfires and why small wins matter. But understanding the psychology of anxiety is only half the battle. The other half is translating that understanding into the actual words you use on a Tuesday night when your loved one is spiraling.

Support is not just what you say. It is when you say it, how you say it, and whether the words lower pressure or raise it.

When you see someone you love terrified of something objectively harmless, your first verbal reflex is usually an attempt to shrink the problem for them. You think you are being comforting, but your words are actually minimizing their reality. The hardest habit to break is the instinct to dismiss the fear.

To be helpful, you have to stop trying to shrink the problem and start validating the weight of it. You have to learn the language of safety. Let us look at five common scenarios to see what helpful support actually sounds like in real life.

2. Five Scenarios: Support in Practice

Scenario 1: Panic in the Car

What is happening: You are driving to a casual dinner with friends. Out of nowhere, your loved one starts taking short, shallow breaths. They grip the door handle and say, "I can't do this. Everyone is going to be looking at me. I'm going to have a panic attack at the table. We have to turn around."

What you want to say: You want to reassure them by pointing out how safe the situation is. You want to say, "Just calm down, it's just Sarah and Mark. It's not a big deal."

Why that backfires: When you say "Just calm down," you are demanding that they instantly shut off a physiological response they cannot control. When you say "It's not a big deal," you are telling them that their massive, terrifying internal experience is being dismissed. They do not hear reassurance; they hear rejection. The panic immediately worsens because now they are ashamed that they are failing to be normal in front of you.

Better words: Take your foot off the gas slightly to slow the car. Say quietly, "That feels really heavy right now, doesn't it? You don't have to trap yourself. We can go in for ten minutes, and if it's too much, I will make an excuse and we will leave. You are in control."

Why this works: You did not dismiss the fear. You validated the weight of it and then offered a concrete exit strategy. By validating the emotion instead of dismissing it, you become a safe harbor.

<u>Scenario 2:</u> Pacing in the Kitchen

What is happening: It is a Sunday morning. Your loved one wakes up, walks into the kitchen, and immediately starts pacing. They will not make eye contact. They are clearly agitated, but nothing specific has happened yet today.

What you want to say: You want to gather data so you can fix the problem. You want to ask, "What's wrong? Are you worried about work tomorrow? Did I do something to make you mad? Talk to me."

Why that backfires: An anxious brain in the middle of a spiral often does not know why it is spiraling. The physical symptoms of anxiety can trigger the anxious thoughts, rather than the other way around. When you barrage them with questions, you are demanding a logical explanation for an illogical physical state. The interrogation feels like an attack, adding massive social pressure to the physical panic. They feel cornered and broken.

Better words: Pour a cup of coffee. Do not ask what is wrong. Say gently, "You look like your motor is running really fast this morning. Do you want me to just sit here with you, or do you want some space?"

Why this works: You are offering connection without demanding an explanation. By giving them permission not to know why they are anxious, you remove the pressure to perform. You validate the physical reality without requiring a psychological diagnosis.

Scenario 3: The Insomnia Spiral

What is happening: It is late at night. Your loved one is lying in bed, staring at the ceiling, trapped in an insomnia spiral. They are worrying aloud about a financial decision they have to make next month.

What you want to say: You are tired. You want to go to sleep. You want to say, "We can't do anything about this at 2 AM. Just go to sleep and we will figure it out tomorrow."

Why that backfires: Telling an anxious person to "just go to sleep" highlights their lack of control over their own brain. It makes them feel like a burden who is keeping you awake. The guilt compounds the anxiety, guaranteeing they will get absolutely no sleep.

Better words: "Your brain is being really loud tonight. I am going to hold your hand until it slows down."

Why this works: It externalizes the anxiety. You are not blaming them for being awake; you are acknowledging that their brain is being uncooperative. Physical touch, like holding a hand, can help regulate a racing nervous system far better than logic at 2 AM.

Scenario 4: The Reassurance Loop

What is happening: They are stuck in a loop of seeking reassurance. They have asked you four times in the last hour if you think their boss is mad at them for a minor typo in an email.

What you want to say: You want to shut down the repetitive questioning. You want to say, "I already told you this. Your boss doesn't care. Stop asking me."

Why that backfires: The reassurance loop is a desperate attempt to find a solid surface in a sea of catastrophic "what-ifs." When you snap at them for asking again, you remove the only solid surface they have. You confirm their deepest fear: that their anxiety makes them unlovable and annoying.

Better words: "I know your brain is looking for a guarantee right now. I still believe your boss is not mad. But I also know my answer isn't turning off the alarm for you."

Why this works: You answer the question, but you also name the mechanism behind the loop. You gently point out that the reassurance is not actually working, which helps them recognize that they are fighting a body alarm, not a real work crisis.

<u>Scenario 5:</u> Shutdown After a Hard Comment

What is happening: You are having a tense conversation about household chores. You make a slightly sharp comment out of frustration. They immediately go silent, pull their knees to their chest, and shut down completely.

What you want to say: You feel defensive. You want to say, "Don't do that. Don't shut down on me just because I asked you to help out more. You are acting like I yelled at you."

Why that backfires: You are punishing them for a freeze response. When they shut down, their nervous system has perceived your sharp comment as a severe threat. Pushing against the freeze response only confirms to their nervous system that the moment is not safe.

Better words: "I am sorry, my tone was too sharp just then. I am frustrated about the chores, but I am not attacking you. Take a minute."

Why this works: You take immediate accountability for your tone, which lowers the threat level. You separate the practical issue (the chores) from their safety in the relationship. You give their nervous system permission to thaw.

3. Common Harmful Phrases

Even with the best intentions, certain phrases have become deeply ingrained in our cultural vocabulary for dealing with stress. When applied to an anxiety disorder, these phrases can do real damage. Here are the most common harmful phrases, what your loved one actually hears, and what you should say instead.

Harmful phrase:
"Just calm down."

What they hear:
"Your physical reality is too much for me, and you need to turn it off immediately."

Better replacement:
"I am right here. Take your time."

Harmful phrase:
"You're overthinking."

What they hear:
"Your fears are not valid, and your reality does not make sense."

Better replacement:
"Your brain is running really fast right now."

Harmful phrase:
"It's not a big deal."

What they hear:
"You are weak for being terrified of something so small."

Better replacement:
"I can see how heavy this feels for you today."

Harmful phrase:
"What's wrong with you?"

What they hear:
"Something is wrong with you at a deeper level."

Better replacement:
"You look like you are fighting a really hard battle right now."

Harmful phrase:
"I already told you this."

What they hear:
"You are annoying me, and I am losing my patience with your need for safety."

Better replacement:
"I know your brain is looking for a guarantee right now."

Harmful phrase:
"You're fine."

What they hear:
"I refuse to see your pain, and you are entirely alone in it."

Better replacement:
"I know you don't feel fine right now. I've got you."

4. The Power of Tone

The exact words you use are important, but they are entirely useless if your tone of voice contradicts them. An anxious brain is hyper-vigilant. It is constantly scanning the environment for threats. It does not just listen to the dictionary definition of your words; it analyzes the pitch, speed, and volume of your delivery.

If your words say "I am here to help," but your tone says "I am exhausted and frustrated by you," the anxious brain will always believe the tone.

You can use the exact same words, but a different tone changes the entire meaning. If you say, "We don't have to solve this right now," with a quick, clipped voice and a heavy sigh, the anxious person hears: You are a burden, and your anxiety is ruining my night.

But if you say those exact same words slowly, softly, and with a relaxed posture, it lands as a comfort rather than a command.

A slow voice is a biological safety signal. It proves to their nervous system that there is no immediate threat in the room. It proves that you are not angry, that they are not a burden, and that the space is safe.

Body language matters just as much. Standing over someone while they are sitting on the couch or lying in bed is inherently dominating. It triggers a primal threat response. If you want your words to land softly, you must physically lower yourself. Sit beside them. Kneel on the floor. Put yourself at eye level or below.

To be truly supportive, your tone and posture must match your words. You have to regulate your own nervous system before you try to soothe theirs.

5. The Importance of Timing

Helpful words can fail completely if they are delivered at the wrong time. You cannot teach a swimming lesson while someone is actively drowning.

During peak panic:
When the body alarm is blaring and they are actively panicking, they cannot process complex sentences. Their auditory processing is compromised. This is not the time for deep, validating conversations. This is the time for short, simple, repetitive safety signals. "I am here." "You are safe." "Breathe with me."

While they are frozen:
When they are in a deep freeze or shutdown, demanding a verbal response from them is a form of pressure. If you ask, "What do you need?" while they are frozen, you are giving them a task they cannot complete. Instead, make statements that require no response. "I am going to sit here and read my book. You don't have to talk."

While you are angry:
If you are deeply frustrated, your tone will betray you. Do not try to offer support while you are actively resenting them. It is far better to step away and say, "I need to take a ten-minute break, but we are okay," than to try and force a supportive script through gritted teeth.

Before the nervous system settles:
Do not try to debrief a panic attack or an anxiety spiral

the moment it ends. The adrenaline crash leaves them exhausted and fragile. Wait until their nervous system has fully settled—often the next day—before you ask, "What happened yesterday?"

6. Mini Script Bank

When you are exhausted and your loved one is spiraling, it is hard to find the right words. Keep these simple scripts in your back pocket for common situations.

When they are panicking:
"I am right here. You are safe. We don't have to fix anything right now."

When they are frozen:
"You look stuck. I am going to sit right here with you. You don't have to talk."

When they ask for reassurance:
"I know your brain is looking for a guarantee. I am still here, and we are still okay."

When they apologize too much:
"You don't have to apologize for having a hard day. You are not a burden to me."

When you are out of capacity:
"I love you, but my battery is completely empty right now. I need to take an hour to recharge, and then I will come back to sit with you."

7. Reader Reflection Exercise

Take a moment to reflect on your own communication habits. Answer these questions honestly:

When my loved one is anxious, do I usually try to shrink the problem or validate the weight of it?

Which of the "Common Harmful Phrases" do I use the most often?

Have I ever interrogated them about why they are anxious when they clearly do not know?

When I am frustrated, how does my tone of voice change? Does it get faster, louder, or sharper?

Do I often sigh or roll my eyes when they ask for reassurance?

Have I ever tried to have a deep conversation while they were actively panicking?

Do I stand over them when they are frozen, or do I sit beside them?

How hard is it for me to accept that my tone matters more than my words?

Do I feel guilty admitting when I am out of capacity to support them?

What is one specific phrase I can completely eliminate from my vocabulary this week?

8. What to Practice This Week

Changing your verbal habits requires intentional practice. Use this five-day plan to start speaking the language of safety.

-Monday: Notice one phrase you use.
Do not try to change your language today. Just listen to yourself. Notice when you use a phrase like "just calm down" or "you're overthinking." Silently acknowledge the instinct to dismiss the fear.

-Tuesday: Slow your voice.
Focus entirely on your delivery today. When you speak to your loved one about anything—even what is for dinner—consciously lower your volume and slow your speaking speed. Notice how a calmer tone changes the energy in the room.

-Wednesday: Replace dismissal with validation.
When they express a fear today, commit to not telling them why they are wrong. Replace the dismissal with validation. Say, "That sounds really heavy," and leave it at that.

-Thursday: Sit beside instead of standing over.
Pay attention to your body language. If they are sitting or lying down and you need to talk to them, do not stand over them. Pull up a chair, sit on the edge of the bed, or kneel on the floor. Put yourself at eye level.

-Friday: Use one script without adding pressure.
Find an opportunity to use one of the scripts from the Mini Script Bank. If they are stuck, say, "You look

stuck. I am going to sit right here with you." Deliver it slowly, and do not demand a response.

Support is not about having all the answers. It is about creating an environment where the anxiety does not have to be fought alone. When you learn to speak the language of safety, you become the solid ground they need to start rebuilding their life.

Chapter 6: The Done List for Loved Ones

1. What the Done List is

The Done List is one of the simplest tools in this whole book. It is exactly what it sounds like: a list of what has already been done, not a list of everything still waiting.

It is not a planner. It is not a schedule. It is not another way to organize pressure. It is a visible record of effort.

For the anxious person, the Done List becomes proof that the day is not empty and that they are not failing at life. For the loved one, it creates a shared language of progress. It gives both of you a way to notice the small, real movements that anxiety usually erases.

That matters because so much of anxiety happens invisibly. You may see a person who did not finish the laundry. They may be living inside a day where they got out of bed, ate something, took medication, answered one message, and fought through three separate spirals without falling apart. The Done List helps make that effort visible.

It bridges the gap between what you see on the outside and what they are carrying on the inside.

2. Why it works differently than a to-do list

To understand why the Done List helps, you first have to understand why traditional to-do lists can become so painful for an anxious brain.

When a non-anxious person looks at a to-do list, they may see a helpful map. The list gives structure. It shows what needs attention. It can make the day feel organized.

But when an anxious person looks at the same list, they may not see a map. They may see a threat report.

Every unchecked box can feel like proof that they are behind. Every unfinished task can feel like evidence that they are unreliable, lazy, disappointing, or failing you. A list with ten unfinished items can become a document showing ten different ways they are not measuring up.

That is why a to-do list can backfire. It gathers everything that has not happened yet and puts it in one place where anxiety can stare at it.

The Done List reverses that pressure. Instead of pointing at what is still waiting, it points at what already happened. It moves the mind from deficit to evidence. It says: something was done. Effort happened here. The day contains movement.

That shift matters. When the nervous system sees only threat, it freezes. When it sees evidence of safety and success, even small success, it has a better chance of loosening. The Done List does not magically cure anxiety. It simply gives the anxious brain better information to work with.

3. Why anxious people forget progress and remember failure

Anxiety is built to scan for danger. Its job is to look for what could go wrong, what might be missed, and what could lead to pain, rejection, embarrassment, failure, or conflict.

In modern life, danger is not usually a predator in the woods. It is the unanswered message. The overdue bill. The disappointed look on someone's face. The phone call that might bring bad news. The task that should have been done yesterday.

Because anxiety is focused on threat, it remembers failure with frightening accuracy. It remembers the task that slipped through. It remembers the time someone sounded irritated. It remembers the appointment that was missed, the chore that was not finished, and the moment they felt embarrassed.

Progress does not always register the same way. Taking a shower may not feel important because it is not a threat. Eating breakfast may disappear from memory because the brain is busy tracking everything still unfinished. Paying one bill may be forgotten as soon as the next bill comes into view.

This is why your loved one can have a productive morning and still break down by midafternoon, convinced the day is ruined. Their anxiety has highlighted what remains undone and deleted the effort that already happened.

The Done List functions like an external memory. It holds onto the evidence anxiety keeps throwing away.

4. How to introduce the Done List without making it feel like a fix-it project

Because you are reading this book, you may feel eager to introduce the Done List right away. You see the logic. You understand the tool. You want your loved one to feel better.

That desire makes sense. But this is also where you need to be careful.

Anxious people are often exhausted by solutions. They may have tried planners, apps, routines, reminders, therapy worksheets, productivity systems, and well-meaning advice. Some of those tools may have helped. Some may have turned into one more place to fail.

So if you walk into the room and announce that you have found the thing that will fix them, the Done List may become another burden before it even begins.

If it feels like a fix, it will be rejected.

The Done List should be introduced as an experiment, not an assignment. It should feel like a gentle option, not a new rule. It should not be presented during a panic attack, a shutdown, an argument, or a moment when the person already feels ashamed.

Introduce it when the room is calm. Introduce it with respect. Introduce it as something that might help them see what is already true, not as something they must do to become acceptable.

5. What to say when introducing it

The goal is to validate their experience first and offer the tool second.

A good moment might be a quiet drive, a calm Sunday morning, or an ordinary evening when nobody is actively spiraling. You are not trying to ambush them with a system. You are opening a conversation.

You might say:

"I was reading about how anxiety can make the brain focus so hard on what is unfinished that it forgets what already got done. Does that ever feel true for you?"

Then stop. Let them answer. Let them tell you whether that fits.

If they say yes, you can continue:

"The book talked about something called a Done List. Instead of writing down what still needs to happen, you only write down what already happened. Even tiny things. Getting up. Eating. Taking medicine. Answering one text. It is not about proving anything.

It is just a way to show your brain that the day is not empty."

Then make it lower pressure:

"I thought it sounded useful. I may even try it myself for work, because I know I forget what I actually finish."

That last part matters. When you make the tool human and ordinary, rather than something only the anxious person needs because they are struggling, you lower shame. You are not saying, "Here is your new anxiety assignment." You are saying, "This is a way people can notice effort more honestly."

6. What not to say

Do not introduce the Done List with urgency, frustration, or project-manager energy.

Do not say:

"You are spiraling again because you keep focusing on everything you have not done. I read about this Done List thing. Sit down and write down what you did today so you can see that you are being dramatic."

That may not be what you intend, but it is what a frustrated introduction can sound like.

This approach fails because it turns the tool into a demand. It tells them their feelings are wrong. It asks them to perform a new task while their nervous system is already overloaded. Now the Done List is associated with your disappointment and their inadequacy.

Also avoid using it as a correction:

"You would feel better if you would just do your Done List."

That sentence takes a tool meant to reduce shame and turns it into another thing they are failing to use properly.

The Done List only works if it remains gentle. The moment it becomes a command, a lecture, or a measure of compliance, it stops being support and starts becoming pressure.

7. How to notice wins without being patronizing

Once the Done List has been introduced, your job is to help your loved one notice effort without making them feel small.

There is a fine line between validating a small win and sounding like you are praising a toddler. The difference is dignity.

Patronizing sounds like this:

"Oh my gosh, sweetie, I am so proud of you for finally taking a shower. Look at you go!"

That may come from love, but it can feel humiliating. It highlights how hard a basic task was and makes the person feel like they are being applauded for barely functioning.

Validating sounds different:

"Hey, I noticed you got a shower in. I know this morning was heavy. I'm glad you got a minute to reset."

That sentence sees the effort without turning it into a performance. It names the context. It respects the person. It does not make them feel like a child.

Your goal is to act as a mirror, not a cheerleader. You are reflecting back what actually happened: effort, movement, follow-through, care.

8. How to celebrate wins in the moment

Celebration matters, but it has to be handled with care. You are not throwing a parade every time they complete a basic task. You are helping their brain register that progress happened.

If they make a phone call they were dreading, you might say:

"That call is done. I know you were carrying it for a while. Good job getting it out of the way."

Then let the win stand.

Do not immediately say, "Now that you did that, maybe you can also call the dentist."

Do not ask, "Do you feel better now?"

Do not turn the win into a doorway to more work.

A win needs room to land. If you immediately attach another expectation to it, the anxious person learns that success only earns them more pressure. That makes future wins feel dangerous.

Celebrate briefly. Be specific. Then move on.

The celebration should communicate: I saw the effort. It counts. You do not have to perform anything else for me right now.

9. How to avoid turning it into a scoreboard

The most dangerous mistake a support person can make is turning the Done List into a management tool.

Because you love them and want to see them succeed, you may want to monitor it. You may want to ask, "Did you write anything down today?" You may want to check the list before bed. You may want to remind them, "Hey, you just did the dishes. Go put that on your Done List."

Be very careful.

The Done List only works if it belongs to the anxious person. It is a tool for self-validation, not external accountability. If you become the manager of the list, the list becomes another expectation they have to meet.

If you monitor the list, you become their boss. An anxious person does not need a boss. They need support.

Your job is to notice wins verbally and respectfully. Their job, if they choose, is to record them. That boundary protects the tool from becoming another form of pressure.

10. What to do when they resist the idea

Not every anxious person will immediately accept the Done List. Some will resist it because the idea of writing down "took a shower" or "ate toast" feels embarrassing. They may believe those things should not count.

They may say:

"That is stupid. I should not need a medal for doing basic adult things."

Do not argue. Do not try to educate harder. Do not defend the tool like you are selling it.

Validate the feeling without agreeing with the shame.

"I get why it feels that way. But I also know your brain is being really mean to you today. You do not have to use the list if you do not want to. I am just going to keep noticing when you do hard things, because I see how much effort it takes."

Then drop it.

This is important. If they resist the tool, do not push the tool. Keep the behavior. Keep noticing effort. Keep naming small wins without making them perform. Over time, they may become more open to writing those wins down themselves.

You can become an external Done List for a while, but quietly. Not by managing them. By noticing truth until they are ready to notice it too.

11. What to do on a hard day

On a truly hard day, the Done List changes shape.

When panic is high and the freeze is deep, the definition of a win drops all the way to the floor. This is not lowering standards because you have given up. It is matching the tool to reality.

On a hard day, a win might be drinking water. Eating toast. Taking medication. Moving from the bed to the couch. Breathing through a panic attack without making it worse. Sending one text that says, "I cannot talk right now."

These are not fake wins. They are survival wins. And survival wins matter.

Your role on a hard day is to lower the bar without making the person feel pathetic.

You might say:

"Today is just about getting through today. Drinking that water counted. Resting counted. We can worry about the rest tomorrow."

That sentence does two things. It releases them from the impossible standard of a normal day, and it protects the dignity of the smaller effort.

Hard days are exactly when the Done List may matter most. Not because it makes the day easy, but because it keeps the day from being erased by shame.

12. Sample loved-one scenarios

Scenario 1: The overwhelmed weekend

What the anxious person experiences: They look at the messy house on Saturday morning and feel completely paralyzed by the volume of cleaning that needs to be done. They sit on the couch, scrolling their phone, hating themselves for not starting.

What the loved one sees: They see their partner ignoring the chores they promised to do and choosing to look at their phone instead.

What the loved one gets wrong: They assume their partner is being lazy or avoiding responsibility.

Mishandled: "Are you seriously just going to sit there all day? I have been cleaning for an hour. You said you would help."

Result: The anxious person shuts down completely, feeling attacked and useless.

Handled well: "The house is a lot today. Let's just pick one tiny thing. Can you gather the trash from the living room? I'll handle the kitchen. We can stop after that."

Result: The task becomes small enough to approach, and the person has a chance to participate without being crushed by the whole house.

Scenario 2: The forgotten win

What the anxious person experiences: They replied to a difficult email in the morning, but by afternoon they are spiraling because dinner is not started. They feel like a failure.

What the loved one sees: They see their partner crying in the kitchen because dinner is not happening.

What the loved one gets wrong: They try to fix the dinner problem instead of addressing the emotional spiral.

Mishandled: "It is fine. I will just order pizza. Don't cry over dinner."

Result: The anxious person feels even more useless because now dinner is another thing they could not manage.

Handled well: "Dinner does not matter right now. Your brain is lying to you again. You handled that massive email this morning, remember? That was a real win. Let's order pizza and call today successful enough."

Result: You remind them of the forgotten win, lower the pressure, and help them see that the day was not empty.

13. Mini scripts for spouses, parents, and friends

For spouses:

"I know your brain is telling you that you have not done enough today. But I saw you handle [Task A] and [Task B]. You are doing better than your anxiety is telling you."

For parents:

"You do not have to figure everything out right now. Let's just focus on the next ten minutes. What is one tiny thing that feels possible?"

For friends:

"I know you are stressed about everything unfinished. But you showed up today, and that counts. Let's grab coffee and reset."

Use these as starting points, not scripts you have to repeat perfectly. Your loved one does not need polished lines. They need language that lowers pressure, protects dignity, and tells the truth about effort.

14. Closing reflection: the Done List belongs to support, not control

The Done List is a mirror, not a leash.

It is a way for your loved one to finally see the effort they are putting into surviving a world that can feel constantly overwhelming. It helps them notice movement that anxiety would otherwise erase.

When you use the language of the Done List, when you notice small wins, validate invisible effort, and refuse to become the manager of their progress, you stop being a source of pressure and become more of a source of safety.

You cannot control their anxiety. You cannot force them to heal. But you can change some of the pressure in the environment where healing is trying to happen.

When the environment feels safer, the nervous system has a better chance of calming down. When the nervous system calms down, the freeze has a better chance of lifting. And when the freeze lifts, momentum can begin.

That is the real power of the Done List.

Chapter 7: How to Help Without Taking Over

1. The boundary between support and control

When you love someone who is struggling with anxiety, your first instinct is often to step in and fix it. You want to carry the weight for them. You want to make the calls, organize the schedule, clean the kitchen, answer the email, and clear the path so they do not have to feel overwhelmed anymore.

That instinct usually comes from care. You are not trying to control them. You are trying to relieve pressure. You want the moment to stop hurting. You want the house to function. You want the thing to be done so both of you can breathe.

But this is where support can quietly become control.

Support stands next to someone while they carry a heavy box. Control takes the box out of their hands because you are afraid they will drop it.

That difference matters. When you take over too quickly, you may solve the immediate problem, but you can also send a painful message to their nervous system: You cannot handle this, so I have to do it for you.

Over time, that message erodes confidence. It can make them more dependent on you to function, not because they want to be dependent, but because their brain starts collecting evidence that they cannot be trusted with hard things.

Your job is not to do every hard thing for them. Your job is to help them discover that hard things can be approached in smaller, safer, more manageable ways.

That is the heart of this chapter. You are not stepping away from them. You are not abandoning them to struggle alone. You are learning how to stay close without taking over.

2. What taking over feels like from the inside

For the anxious person, having someone take over a task can feel like relief and shame arriving at the same time.

The relief is real. The dreaded phone call is made. The bill is paid. The kitchen gets cleaned. The email gets sent. The immediate pressure disappears. For a few minutes, their body may relax because the threat has been removed.

But underneath that relief, something heavier often begins to form.

They watch you complete the task quickly, calmly, and efficiently. The thing that had them paralyzed for three days takes you five minutes. You may think that proves the task was simple. Their anxiety uses it to prove they are broken.

Why could they do it so easily?

Why could I not just handle that?

What is wrong with me?

That is the danger of taking over. It can relieve the symptom while strengthening the belief that they are incapable.

The unfinished task was not the whole problem. The deeper problem was their fear that they cannot handle ordinary life. When you take the task away too quickly, they lose the chance to gather evidence against that fear.

They need to experience some friction, then experience some success. Not all the friction. Not a crushing amount. Not the whole task when the whole task is too much. But some small part they can survive.

That is how confidence comes back. Not because someone tells them they are capable, but because they feel themselves do one small thing and live through it.

3. What taking over looks like from the outside

From your side, taking over can feel like the only reasonable option.

You see the laundry sitting there. You see the bill getting closer to the due date. You see the form half-finished on the table. You see the groceries that need to be bought, the dog that needs to be walked, the child who needs to be picked up, the dinner that needs to happen whether anxiety is present or not.

You are tired too. You may have already been patient. You may have asked gently. You may have waited all day. At some point, efficiency starts to look like kindness.

You think, I can just do this faster.

And you probably can.

That is the trap.

Taking over is efficient. It gets the visible task done. But if it becomes the default pattern, it prioritizes completion over capacity.

You have to decide what you are trying to build. Are you trying to get the laundry folded today, or are you trying to help your loved one slowly rebuild the ability to face laundry tomorrow? Sometimes the answer will be both. Sometimes an urgent task really does need to be handled. But if you always choose speed, you may accidentally teach their nervous system that they are not needed in their own life.

Support is slower than control. It often looks less impressive from the outside. It may mean the kitchen takes longer, the email gets written in pieces, and the grocery list has only three items on it instead of the full week of meals.

But slow support gives something control cannot give: agency.

4. The stop-on-a-high-note guardrail

One of the most common mistakes loved ones make is pushing for more once momentum begins.

If your loved one finally gets off the couch and washes one dish, your instinct may be to say, "Great. Now let's do the rest of the sink."

That instinct makes sense. You see motion and want to build on it. You want to use the opening while it is there. But for an anxious person, that can turn a small victory into a warning.

Their brain learns: If I do one thing, they will expect ten things.

That makes starting feel dangerous next time.

Momentum must not become a marathon. When an anxious person breaks through the freeze response, the energy they find is often fragile. If you immediately raise the expectation, you turn relief into pressure. You take the small win they just earned and attach a new demand to it.

This is why the stop-on-a-high-note guardrail matters.

When they complete one small task, celebrate the win and explicitly give them permission to stop.

"Hey, you got the dishwasher loaded. That is a real win. Let's stop there for now. You do not need to do the counters."

That sentence does more than end the task. It teaches their nervous system that action does not always lead to punishment, escalation, or endless demand. It teaches them that they can do one thing and still be safe.

Stopping early can feel strange to you. You may think, But they are finally moving. Why would we stop now?

Because you are not only trying to finish today's chore. You are trying to make tomorrow's attempt feel possible.

5. Shared tasks without taking over

Consider a grocery run.

The fridge is empty. The week is starting. Someone needs to go to the store.

Your loved one knows this. They are not unaware of the problem. They may be sitting on the couch, scrolling their phone, while their mind loops through the crowded aisles, the fluorescent lights, the decisions, the checkout line, the possibility of forgetting something important, and the shame of needing help with something other people seem to do without thinking.

From the outside, you see avoidance. You see your partner leaving the physical work to you again.

The mishandled version sounds like this:

"Fine, I'll just go do it myself. You stay here and relax. I'll handle everything like I always do."

That gets the groceries bought. It also builds resentment in you and shame in them. They hear that they are useless. You feel abandoned. The grocery run becomes another brick in the wall between you.

The handled-well version protects agency while still being realistic.

"Hey, I know the store feels like a lot today. I'm going to do the shopping. Can you write down three things we need for dinners this week? I'll handle the rest."

That response matters because you are taking on the heaviest part of the task without erasing their contribution. You are not pretending the store is easy. You are not forcing them into a crowded environment when they are already overwhelmed. But you are also not removing them from the household entirely.

They still contribute. They still choose three things. They still participate in the life you share.

That is scaffolding.

Scaffolding means you provide enough support for them to stay involved, but not so much support that they disappear from the process.

6. The dreaded phone call

Phone calls are a common place where support turns into control.

Imagine your loved one needs to call the insurance company to fix a billing error. The thought of being on hold, explaining the issue, arguing with a representative, and possibly crying in frustration has kept them from making the call for three weeks.

You see the bill. You see the deadline. You see the risk of collections. Your urgency is understandable.

The mishandled response is direct takeover.

"Give me the phone. I'm just going to call them right now and get this sorted out. It is ridiculous that you have put this off for so long."

The bill may get handled. But your loved one is likely left feeling infantilized, embarrassed, and less capable of making the next call.

The handled-well response gives support without stealing the action.

"That insurance call is hanging over your head, isn't it? I know those calls are the worst. How about I sit right here while you dial? I can look up the account number, and if you get stuck, I am right here. We can get ice cream after."

This keeps agency intact. You are not abandoning them to the call. You are also not removing them from it. You provide presence, help with the account number, and a small reward after the task. They still dial. They still speak. They still experience themselves surviving the call.

That experience matters more than a perfectly efficient phone call.

7. Leaving the house without forcing the door

Leaving the house can become another battleground between support and control.

Suppose you are supposed to leave for a friend's birthday party in twenty minutes. Your loved one is standing in the closet, staring at their clothes, completely frozen. The idea of small talk, noise, perceived judgment, and being trapped in a group setting is crushing them.

From the outside, you may see someone dragging their feet and making you late again.

The mishandled version sounds like this:

"Just put on the blue shirt. It looks fine. We are going to be late. Put your shoes on. I'm starting the car."

That may get them out the door, but it does not make them feel safe. It shoves them into a high-stress environment while they are already panicked. They may spend the whole event counting the minutes until they can leave. The next invitation will feel even heavier.

The handled-well version gives them a real choice and a safe exit.

"Hey, you look stuck. Do you want to go, or is the idea of a big group too much right now? If we go, we can set a timer and leave after forty-five minutes. If we stay, we can order takeout. Your call."

This response gives agency back to the anxious person. You are not making the choice for them. You are not shaming them for being stuck. You are creating two acceptable options.

The forty-five-minute exit strategy also lowers the threat level. A party with no exit may feel impossible. A party with a clear, honored exit may become possible.

Sometimes the most supportive thing you can say is not "You have to go." It is "You are allowed to leave."

8. Tips for shared agency

Shared agency is the middle path between abandonment and control. You are not leaving your loved one alone with a task that feels impossible. You are also not taking the task away before they have a chance to try.

Here are the core practices that keep support helpful.

Offer choices, not commands.

Anxiety strips a person of their feeling of control. Commands can make that worse. Instead of "Go take a shower," try, "Do you want to shower before dinner or after dinner?" A choice gives their brain something small to decide. That small decision helps rebuild agency.

Share the load, but do not seize the task.

If the kitchen is a disaster, do not banish them from the room while you clean it. Ask for one specific, bounded contribution. "I'm going to load the dishwasher. Can you wipe down the island?" That lets the task become shared without making them disappear.

Let them do it imperfectly.

If they are finally folding laundry, do not correct the towels. If they are making the phone call, do not whisper instructions in their ear. The goal is not perfect execution. The goal is completion with dignity. Correcting them mid-task often triggers shame and makes them less likely to try again.

Praise effort, not speed.

An anxious brain may move slowly through tasks that feel threatening. If it takes forty-five minutes to write a three-sentence email, do not point out the time. Notice the persistence. "You stayed with that even though it was hard. That counts."

Stop before the crash.

Encourage them to stop while they still have a little energy left. If they push until they are completely depleted, their brain may connect the task with exhaustion and dread. Stopping before the crash makes it easier to return tomorrow.

Ask before stepping in.

If you see them struggling, do not assume they want rescue. Ask. "You look stuck on that form. Do you want me to read the instructions, or do you want to keep trying for a few more minutes?" That question respects both their struggle and their adulthood.

These practices may seem small, but they change the entire emotional tone of help. The point is not to make everything easy. The point is to make hard things survivable without stripping away dignity.

9. When they resist scaffolding

Sometimes, when you offer scaffolding instead of taking over, your loved one may get angry.

They may say, "If you are going to sit there and watch me do it, why don't you just do it yourself?"

That reaction can sting. You are trying to help. You are trying not to take over. You are doing the thing this book is telling you to do, and now they seem angry at you for it.

But that anger is often fear wearing armor.

They may be afraid they will fail in front of you. They may feel exposed by needing help. They may want you to do the task because being watched while struggling feels unbearable.

The mishandled response is to take the anger personally.

"Fine. I'm just trying to help you. If you want to sit there and stare at the wall, go ahead. I'll do it myself since you clearly can't."

Now the argument escalates. Their fear of incompetence is confirmed. Your frustration rises. The task becomes a battlefield.

The handled-well response validates the frustration without taking the bait.

"I know this is frustrating, and I'm not trying to be difficult. I just know that when I do it for you, it tends to make you feel worse later. I'm right here. We can do it together, or we can put it away and try again tomorrow."

This response holds two truths at once. You are not abandoning them, and you are not rescuing them. You are staying present while protecting the boundary that the task cannot automatically become yours just because anxiety got loud.

That balance may not feel graceful at first. It may feel awkward. They may still be irritated. But you are teaching a new pattern, and new patterns often feel strange before they feel safe.

10. When they completely shut down

There will be days when scaffolding does not work.

There will be days when anxiety is so heavy that your loved one cannot make a choice, cannot complete even the smallest part of the task, and cannot respond to the kindest version of help.

When that happens, you have to make a practical judgment.

If the task is not urgent, let it go. Laundry can wait. The closet can wait. The nonessential errand can wait. Do not turn a non-urgent task into an emotional emergency just because you are tired of seeing it undone.

If the task is urgent, you may have to take over. The dog needs to be fed. A child needs to be picked up. A critical bill may need to be paid today. Real life still exists, and support does not mean pretending consequences do not matter.

When you must take over during a total shutdown, do it quietly.

Do not sigh heavily. Do not slam cabinet doors. Do not make a performance of your effort. The anxious person is already drowning in guilt. Performing your frustration only pushes them deeper into the freeze.

Do not bring it up later as evidence against them.

When the crisis has passed and their nervous system has settled, do not use the task as a weapon. Do not say, "Well, I had to pay the electric bill yesterday because you were having a meltdown." The task is done. Let it stay done.

Then return to agency when they settle.

Do not assume that because they shut down yesterday, they need you to take over today. The next calm moment is a chance to return to choices, shared tasks, small steps, and the Done List. Always come back to capacity when capacity returns.

Taking over in an emergency does not mean the whole method failed. It means you handled the emergency. The work resumes when the nervous system has room to participate again.

11. Building capacity takes time

Taking over is fast. Scaffolding is slow.

When you choose support instead of control, you are choosing the longer, harder path. It requires patience. It requires watching someone you love struggle with a task you could finish in seconds. It requires biting your tongue when they do it inefficiently. It requires tolerating the discomfort of slow progress.

But this slow path is the one that builds capacity.

Every time you provide scaffolding instead of rescue, you help them lay one small brick in the foundation of their confidence. You are not only helping with laundry, phone calls, groceries, or paperwork. You are helping them gather evidence that they can survive the friction of ordinary life.

That evidence matters.

Anxiety says, You cannot handle this.

Scaffolding says, Let's find the part you can handle.

Over time, that difference changes more than the task. It changes the way your loved one experiences themselves.

You are not there to become their manager. You are not there to become their rescuer. You are there to become a steady place where effort can happen without shame.

That is how helping becomes support instead of control.

Chapter 8: Hard Days, Good Days, and Setbacks

1. The Myth of the Straight Line

When you are supporting someone through anxiety, your deepest hope is that every day will be a little better than the last. You want to see a clear line of progress. You want the new tool, the new therapist, the new routine, or the new understanding to become the turning point where everything finally clicks and the struggle begins to fade.

That hope makes sense. You love them. You are tired. You want relief for them, and you want relief for yourself too. After a few good days, it is natural to think, Maybe this is it. Maybe we are finally past the worst of it.

But anxiety does not move in a straight line.

Progress often looks jagged. It rises, drops, steadies, dips again, then rises in a way you did not expect. A good day does not guarantee a good week. A breakthrough on Tuesday does not mean they will not be frozen on the couch by Thursday. A better morning does not mean the whole nervous system has changed overnight.

This can be one of the hardest truths for loved ones to accept, because the unevenness feels personal. When they do well, you relax. When they crash, you feel disappointed, scared, or even betrayed by the hope you allowed yourself to feel. You may think, We were doing so well. What happened?

Usually, nothing dramatic happened. Their capacity changed. Their nervous system ran out of fuel. A trigger landed harder than expected. A good day cost more than either of you realized.

If you expect a straight line, every dip will feel like failure. You will feel like the tools are not working, they will feel like they ruined everything, and both of you will panic at the exact moment steadiness is needed most.

Understanding the difference between a hard day, a good day, and a setback protects both of you. It helps you stop treating every dip like a disaster. It helps your loved one stop treating every hard day like proof that nothing is changing.

2. What a Hard Day Looks Like

A hard day is not just a day when your loved one feels sad or stressed. A hard day is a day when their nervous system is running the show. The freeze response is strong. Planning, prioritizing, and following through may be almost impossible.

On a hard day, they may stare at the wall for hours. They may snap at you over something small. They may cancel plans they were excited about yesterday. They may cry because they dropped a spoon. They may sit in the same place all morning, aware of everything that needs to be done and unable to make their body begin.

From the outside, a hard day can look like regression. It can look like they forgot everything they learned. It can look like they stopped caring. It can look like the old pattern is back and all the progress has disappeared.

From the inside, a hard day feels like trying to walk through wet concrete while wearing a weighted vest. Every small action takes more effort than it should. The brain is loud. The body is tired. The fear may not even have a clear object. It is just there, pressing down on everything.

This is where loved ones often make the day harder without meaning to. You see them stuck and want to get them moving. You ask what is wrong. You remind them what needs to happen. You compare today to yesterday. You try to pull them back into the version of themselves you saw on a better day.

But a hard day is not solved by demanding the better version back. A hard day is handled by lowering the bar to match reality.

On a hard day, success may be water, food, medication, a shower, or simply making it through without adding another layer of shame. That may feel like too little to you. To them, it may be the entire day's work.

When you understand that, your response changes. You stop asking, How do I get them back to normal today? You start asking, How do I help today become less damaging? That is a much kinder and more useful question.

3. What a Good Day Looks Like and the Danger It Hides

A good day is a relief. The freeze lifts. Your loved one has energy. They make the phone calls, clean part of the house, laugh at jokes, answer messages, and seem more like the person you remember before anxiety took up so much space.

A good day can feel like a door opening. You want to run through it. You want to believe the hard season is finally ending. Your loved one may want that too. In fact, they may want it so badly that they try to make the good day do too much.

This is where good days become risky.

When an anxious person finally has energy, they often try to make up for all the hard days at once. They clean the house, answer every message, run errands, reorganize the closet, say yes to plans, and stay up late trying to prove they are okay. They are not only enjoying the energy. They are trying to outrun the shame they felt when they had none.

That energy can look wonderful from the outside. You may think, This is what we have been waiting for. You may encourage it without realizing what is happening. You may say, Since you are already up, do you want to tackle the garage too? Or, You are doing so great today, maybe we should finally get all of this done.

That encouragement can come from love, but it can push them straight into a crash.

A good day may be running on borrowed energy. If they spend every bit of it trying to catch up, tomorrow may be brutal. Their nervous system may hit empty. Then they wake up frozen again, ashamed again, and convinced that yesterday's progress was fake.

Your role on a good day is not to squeeze as much productivity out of it as possible. Your role is to protect the good day from becoming a punishment.

This is where the stop-on-a-high-note rule matters. Celebrate what got done. Let it count. Then help them stop before they are empty. The goal is not to do everything while the window is open. The goal is to teach their nervous system that movement can happen without ending in collapse.

4. How Setbacks Happen

A setback is different from a hard day. A hard day is a temporary dip in capacity. A setback is a longer return to old patterns. It may last several days, a week, or longer. The Done List may stop getting used. The small wins may feel invisible again. The house may get heavier. The shame may get louder.

Setbacks usually happen for a reason, even when the reason is not immediately obvious.

Sometimes the setback comes after a sprint. Your loved one had several good days, pushed too hard, and completely drained their reserves. What looks like a sudden collapse may actually be the bill coming due for borrowed energy.

Sometimes the setback comes from an external trigger. A stressful email, a family conflict, a medical bill, a work problem, or a social situation may overload their ability to cope. One thing lands, and the nervous system treats it like everything is unsafe again.

Sometimes the setback begins with shame. They have one hard day, then decide that hard day means they failed. The shame becomes heavier than the original anxiety. Instead of resting and returning, they spiral into the belief that all progress is gone.

When a setback happens, your own fear will probably rise. You may think, We are back to square one. You may want to push, correct, lecture, or force the tools back into place. But panic is one of the worst responses you can bring to a setback. Panic tells their nervous system that the situation is an emergency. It confirms the feeling that something terrible is happening.

A setback needs steadiness, not alarm. It needs a return to basics. Water. Food. Sleep. One small win. One calm sentence. One reminder that this is a pause, not a permanent destination.

5. Asking for More on a Good Day

Imagine it is Saturday morning. Your loved one wakes up feeling surprisingly light. The freeze is gone. They start cleaning the kitchen, doing laundry, and organizing the mail. They are moving quickly, almost urgently, trying to fix everything before the anxiety returns.

From the inside, they are not simply being productive. They are trying to prove they are not broken. They are trying to make up for the days when they could not move. They are trying to become useful enough to quiet the shame.

From the outside, you see initiative. You see the person you have missed. You feel encouraged, relieved, and maybe a little excited. The chores that have been sitting around all week are finally getting done.

This is where the mistake happens. You mistake a burst of shame-driven energy for sustainable recovery, and you ask for more.

You say, "It is so great to see you up and moving. The kitchen looks amazing. Hey, since you are already in a cleaning mood, do you want to finally sort out the hall closet?"

They say yes, because they want to keep pleasing you. They want to keep proving they are okay. They want the good day to stay good. But inside, their energy is already thinning out. By the time they finish the closet, they are depleted. By Sunday morning, they are frozen again, and the shame starts over.

The handled-well version sounds different.

You see the clean kitchen. You see the laundry started. You feel that same relief. But instead of adding another task, you protect the win.

"The kitchen looks amazing," you say. "You have done so much this morning. I know you probably want to keep going, but let's stop here for now. Let's protect some energy for tomorrow. Come sit down."

That response does not kill momentum. It protects it. You are acting as the brakes when their shame wants to become the gas pedal. You validate the effort, but you do not turn effort into a demand for more.

Good days should teach the nervous system that movement can be safe. They should not teach it that movement always leads to exhaustion.

6. The Crash After a Good Weekend

Now imagine Monday morning after a good weekend. Your loved one socialized, cleaned, laughed, answered messages, and felt almost normal. You went to bed Sunday night feeling hopeful.

Then Monday comes, and they cannot get out of bed.

From the inside, they feel like a fraud. They remember how well they did over the weekend and cannot understand why they are frozen now. They think, I proved I could do it. So why can't I do it today? What is wrong with me?

From the outside, you may see the exact behavior that scared and frustrated you before. It looks like the progress disappeared overnight. You may feel disappointed, angry, or afraid.

The mishandled response comes from that fear.

"Are you seriously doing this again?" you say. "You were doing so well this weekend. Why are you throwing it all away? Just get up."

That response confirms their worst fear: that their progress was fragile, that they are a disappointment, and that you now regret believing in them. The shame deepens the freeze.

The handled-well response names the crash without treating it like failure.

"Hey," you say quietly. "You went really hard this weekend. You did a lot. It makes sense that your brain needs a minute to recover today. Today is a rest day. We are not going backward. You are just tired."

That sentence removes the accusation. It explains the crash as recovery, not failure. It helps your loved one see that today's exhaustion does not erase yesterday's effort.

The goal is not to pretend the crash is easy. The goal is to keep the crash from becoming a shame spiral. Rest after effort is not regression. Sometimes it is the price of having tried.

7. The External Trigger

Setbacks can also happen when something external hits the nervous system too hard. It may be one email, one bill, one conversation, or one unexpected change in plans. To you, the trigger may look small. To them, it may feel like the floor dropped out.

Imagine your loved one receives an unexpected email from their boss. The message is not openly hostile. It may only ask for a meeting or request clarification on something. But their nervous system reads it as danger. Within minutes, they shut down. They cancel the evening plans. They retreat to the couch and can barely speak.

From the outside, this looks like overreacting. You may think, It is just an email. The boss is not even mad. We have reservations in an hour. Why is this ruining the whole night?

The mishandled response tries to logic the threat away.

"It is just an email," you say. "Your boss is not even mad. You are completely overreacting. We have reservations in an hour. You need to snap out of it."

That response does not calm the nervous system. It adds another threat. Now their brain is afraid of the boss and afraid of disappointing you. The freeze intensifies.

The handled-well response validates the body response without agreeing with the catastrophic story.

"That email really threw you, didn't it?" you say. "I know your brain is telling you it is a disaster right now. Let's just pause. We can cancel the reservations. We will sit here for a bit until the panic passes. The email can wait until tomorrow."

You are not saying the boss email is truly a disaster. You are saying the panic is real. That distinction matters. You do not have to agree with the fear to respect the intensity of it.

By removing the secondary pressure of the dinner reservation, you make room for their nervous system to settle. Once the body is calmer, the email can be handled with more clarity.

8. What Not to Do During a Setback

When a setback occurs, your own anxiety may spike. You may feel desperate to regain control of the situation. That desperation can lead you straight into responses that make the setback worse.

Do not lecture. When someone is frozen, their brain cannot process a speech about how they need to use their coping skills. Even if everything you are saying is technically true, it will land as noise and pressure.

Do not compare them to last week. "But you were doing so well on Thursday" is not encouraging. It highlights the distance between who they were then and who they feel like now. It turns a better day into evidence against them.

Do not call it regression. That word implies that all previous progress has been erased. Use gentler and more accurate language: pause, rest, crash, reset, or recharging. The words you choose shape the emotional meaning of the moment.

Do not make them prove they are still trying. If they are in a deep freeze, forcing one small task just to reassure yourself is not support. It turns their recovery into a performance for your comfort.

During a setback, your first job is not to measure progress. Your first job is to reduce damage. Lower the pressure. Keep the environment steady. Let the nervous system come down before you ask for movement.

9. Practical Scripts for the Highs and Lows

Having the right words ready can prevent you from reacting out of fear or frustration. You do not need perfect language. You need language that lowers pressure, protects dignity, and keeps the next step small.

For a hard day, try: "I can see today is really heavy. You do not have to explain it. Let's drop the expectations for today. Drinking water and resting is enough."

For a crash after a good day, try: "Your brain is exhausted because you worked hard yesterday. This is not a step backward. It is the hangover from a good day. Rest is part of the process."

For a setback, try: "I know it feels like we are back at the beginning, but we are not. Your nervous system hit a wall. We are going to wait right here until it settles down. There is no rush."

For resistance to the Done List during a low point, try: "You do not have to write anything down today. I know it feels pointless right now. I am just going to keep noticing the hard things you do, and we can pick the list back up when you are ready."

These scripts are not magic spells. They will not instantly make anxiety disappear. Their purpose is simpler than that. They keep you from adding shame. They remind your loved one that a hard day does not cost them your steadiness.

10. Today Is Just Today

The most important phrase you can internalize when supporting an anxious person is this: Today is just today. It does not predict tomorrow.

When your loved one is having a hard day, anxiety will tell them that every day for the rest of their life will feel exactly like this. It will tell them the progress was fake. It will tell them the tools do not work. It will tell them they should stop hoping.

If you panic, you strengthen that story. You confirm the fear that this hard day is permanent.

Your job is to be an anchor to reality. You hold the perspective they cannot currently access. You remind them, calmly and consistently, that a bad Tuesday is just a bad Tuesday. It is not a life sentence. It is weather passing through the nervous system.

This does not mean you minimize the pain. It does not mean you say, "Tomorrow will be fine," when you do not know that. It means you refuse to let today become a prophecy.

Today may be hard. Today may be slow. Today may require a lower bar than either of you wanted. But today is still only today. That truth can keep a setback from becoming a collapse.

11. The Power of Steadiness

Supporting someone through anxiety is not quick work. You will watch them take three steps forward and two steps back more than once. It will test your patience. It will bring up your own fear. There will be moments when you want to yell, Just be normal, even if you never say it out loud.

That does not make you cruel. It makes you tired. But tired is exactly when steadiness matters most.

You cannot prevent every hard day. You cannot fix every setback. You cannot guarantee that tomorrow will be easier than today. What you can offer is a response that does not make the low point lower.

Every time you help them move through a hard day without adding shame, you make return easier. Every time you help them pace a good day, you protect the possibility of another one. Every time you refuse to treat a setback like the end of the story, you help keep the door open for the next small step.

Your steadiness is not a cure. It is not your job to become the whole foundation of their healing. But your calm, predictable response can make the environment safer for healing to happen.

When their internal world is chaotic, steadiness becomes a kind of lighthouse. It does not stop the storm. It helps them remember there is still a shore.

Chapter 9: Caring for Yourself While You Support Someone Else

1. The blunt reality of caregiver burnout

If you have been supporting an anxious person for any significant length of time, you are likely exhausted. You may have opened this book looking for ways to help them, but there is another truth underneath that. You may also be looking for a way to stop carrying so much by yourself.

We need to be honest about this: supporting someone through severe anxiety can be draining. It can be lonely. It can be deeply frustrating.

You are allowed to be frustrated. You are allowed to be tired of the canceled plans, the sudden mood shifts, the repeated reassurance, and the constant need to manage the emotional temperature of the room. Feeling that frustration does not make you a bad partner, parent, family member, or friend. It makes you a human being with a nervous system of your own.

Caregiver burnout is not proof that you do not love them enough. It is what happens when you keep pouring out energy without refilling any of it. If you continue to prioritize their stability while ignoring your own, you will eventually run out of capacity. And when you run out, the relationship suffers. Burning out helps no one.

2. The unfair reality of support

There is an unfairness built into being the support person. When the anxious person is spiraling, their nervous system may be hijacking their logic. They may be irrational, demanding, pessimistic, or convinced that everything is falling apart.

In those moments, you often cannot meet their emotion with the same level of emotion. If they panic and you panic back, the room gets louder. If they lash out and you lash back, the freeze deepens. If they are scared and you respond with fear, their brain treats the situation as even more dangerous.

The unfair reality is that, in the middle of a crisis, you may have to bottle your own frustration temporarily. You may have to be the calm adult in the room, even when you want to scream. You may have to regulate your own nervous system while also trying not to add more pressure to theirs.

That is a tremendous amount of emotional labor.

Bottling frustration temporarily can be necessary during an active spiral. But bottling it forever is not noble. It is dangerous. If you never have a safe place to unpack what you are carrying, that swallowed frustration will eventually turn into resentment, numbness, or an explosion you did not mean to have.

3. What burnout looks and feels like

Burnout rarely announces itself with one dramatic collapse. It usually creeps in slowly, disguised as irritation, apathy, avoidance, and guilt. You may not realize you are burned out until you begin recognizing yourself in the warning signs.

Resentment may show up first. You start keeping a mental scorecard of everything you do for them compared with everything they are able to do for you. You notice every chore, every canceled plan, every accommodation, every moment you had to swallow your own needs because theirs felt louder.

Numbness can follow. You watch them cry or panic, and instead of feeling empathy, you feel a cold, hollow exhaustion. Then you feel ashamed because you think, How can I look at someone I love in pain and feel nothing?

Avoidance may begin to look reasonable. You stay at work a little later than necessary. You sit in the car in the driveway for twenty minutes before coming inside. You run one more errand because you are not ready to walk back into the emotional weight of the house.

Snapping becomes easier. Your fuse gets shorter. A simple question, a minor complaint, or one more moment of panic can trigger anger that feels much bigger than the situation in front of you.

Escape fantasies may appear. You catch yourself imagining getting in the car and driving away. Not because you do not love them, but because some part of you is desperate for quiet.

Then comes guilt. You feel guilty for feeling resentful, guilty for needing space, guilty for wanting the anxiety to stop affecting your life, guilty for being human.

That numbness and resentment are frightening, but they are not moral failures. They are warning signs. Your nervous system is telling you, We cannot process any more of this without support. We are full.

4. The danger of the Fixer identity

Many loved ones fall into the trap of tying their own worth to the anxious person's recovery. If the anxious person has a good day, you feel successful. If they have a setback, you feel like you failed.

This is the Fixer identity, and it is dangerous.

When you become the Fixer, you slowly lose your own boundaries. You stop going to the gym because they might need you. You stop seeing friends because you feel guilty leaving them alone. You stop working on your own goals because every spare bit of energy goes into monitoring their anxiety, managing their environment, or trying to keep the next spiral from happening.

The problem is not that you care. The problem is that you have made yourself responsible for something you cannot fully control.

You must separate your identity from their anxiety. Their recovery is not a report card on your love. Their hard day is not proof that you failed. Their setback does not mean you did not try hard enough.

You are a support system, not a savior. Your job is to show up with steadiness, compassion, honesty, and boundaries. It is not to become the manager of their entire inner world.

5. Mishandled vs. handled well: the empty tank

Scenario: The late-night panic

What the loved one experiences: It is 11:00 PM. You have had a grueling day at work, cooked dinner, cleaned the kitchen, answered messages, and handled responsibilities all day. You are desperate for sleep. Then your loved one begins spiraling about an upcoming appointment and needs reassurance.

What the anxious person sees: They are drowning in panic and reaching for the person who usually helps them feel anchored.

What the loved one gets wrong: You try to force yourself to provide support when you have absolutely no capacity left. That effort fails, and the exhaustion turns into an explosion.

Mishandled example: "I cannot do this right now. I have been working all day. I am exhausted. Can you just be okay for one single night so I can sleep?"

Result: You snap out of pure depletion. The anxious person feels attacked and abandoned. The panic escalates into a fight, and now no one sleeps.

Handled well example: "I can see how much you are hurting right now, and I want to support you. But my brain is completely empty. I have nothing useful left to give tonight. I need to sleep so I can be a steadier partner tomorrow. We will talk about this in the morning."

Result: You set a firm boundary without denying their pain. It may be uncomfortable in the moment, but it prevents the bigger rupture that comes when you keep trying to give from an empty tank.

6. Mishandled vs. handled well: the canceled plans

Scenario: The resentful stay-at-home

What the loved one experiences: You have plans to attend a friend's barbecue. You have been looking forward to it all week. An hour before leaving, your anxious loved one freezes and says they cannot go.

What the anxious person sees: They are paralyzed by social anxiety and feel terrible for ruining the plan.

What the loved one gets wrong: You cancel your own plans to stay home and manage their anxiety, but you do it resentfully. The sacrifice becomes punishment.

Mishandled example: "Fine. I will text them and say we are not coming. Again. I guess we are just never leaving the house." You stay home, angry and silent, watching TV on the other side of the couch.

Result: You give up your social outlet and punish them with passive aggression. They feel guilty. You feel trapped. Both people become lonelier.

Handled well example: "I know the barbecue feels like too much for you today. That is okay. You stay here and rest. I have been really looking forward to seeing everyone, so I am going to go for a couple of hours. I will bring you back a plate."

Result: You protect your own need for connection without shaming them for their limit. They are allowed to stay home, and you are allowed to have a life.

7. Mishandled vs. handled well: the explosion

<u>Scenario:</u> The bottled frustration

What the loved one experiences: You have been walking on eggshells for three weeks during a prolonged setback. You have done the chores, managed the crises, adjusted plans, and swallowed your frustration. Then the anxious person complains that you bought the wrong brand of coffee.

What the anxious person sees: They are making a small complaint about coffee.

What the loved one gets wrong: You allow a minor trigger to detonate weeks of unspoken resentment.

Mishandled example: "Are you kidding me? I do everything around here. I pay the bills, I clean the house, I manage your constant meltdowns, and now you are complaining about coffee? You are completely ungrateful."

Result: You unload valid frustration in a weaponized way. The anxious person is crushed by the sudden realization of how much resentment you have been hiding. You may feel guilty afterward, but the damage has already been done.

Handled well example: You feel the explosion coming. You set the coffee down. "I am feeling incredibly overwhelmed and frustrated right now, and it is not just about the coffee. I need to step outside for twenty minutes before I say something unkind."

Result: You recognize your redline before it turns into damage. You remove yourself from the situation, not to punish them, but to protect both of you from the fallout.

8. A practical reset plan for when you snap

Even with the best intentions, you are human. You will eventually snap. You will yell, say something harsh, go cold, or handle a situation poorly. When that happens, do not spiral into your own shame. Shame does not repair anything. Use a reset plan.

Step away. Physically remove yourself from the room before more damage is done. Do not try to fix the argument while your body is still flooded with adrenaline.

Regulate your body. Do not sit and replay the argument over and over. Walk fast. Splash cold water on your face. Drink water. Breathe slowly. Do something that tells your nervous system the emergency is passing.

Vent somewhere safe. Text a trusted friend, write the ugly thoughts in your phone, go to the gym, sit in the car and say the words out loud where no one else has to absorb them. Get the unfair thoughts out somewhere they will not poison your return.

Come back when calm. Do not return just because five minutes passed. Return when your heart rate is lower, your voice can stay quiet, and you are no longer looking for a fight.

Repair the rupture. You do not have to apologize for having a boundary, but you should repair the way you expressed it. You might say, "I was really frustrated earlier, but I should not have yelled. I am sorry for how I said that. I am very tired today, and I need to reset before we keep talking."

Repair does not mean pretending nothing happened. It means taking responsibility for your delivery while still honoring the truth that you have limits.

9. The necessity of healthy outlets

You cannot survive supporting an anxious person if your entire life revolves around their anxiety. You need places where you can step out of the caregiving role and become a full person again. These outlets are not luxuries. They are part of how you keep your own nervous system from living in constant emergency mode.

Physical release matters. Stress builds in the body. If you are constantly de-escalating, monitoring, swallowing frustration, and adjusting plans, that energy has to go somewhere. The gym, running, hiking, lifting weights, yard work, or even a fast walk can help move some of that stress out of your body.

A trusted friend matters. You need someone you can talk to without turning your loved one into a villain. This should be someone steady enough to let you vent without feeding bitterness. You need space to say, "This is hard," and hear, "Of course it is."

Support groups can matter. There is a specific loneliness that comes from supporting someone with severe anxiety. Being around people who understand the exhaustion, guilt, love, and frustration can help you feel less isolated.

Therapy can matter. If the anxiety in your home is severe, you may need your own professional support. You need a place where you can say the ugly, exhausted things you cannot say to your loved one during a spiral. You need help protecting your own boundaries before resentment makes them for you.

Time alone matters. You need time when you are not responsible for anyone else's emotional state. That may mean a drive, a quiet room, a workout, a walk, a hobby, or thirty minutes where nobody needs anything from you. Alone time is not abandonment. It is recovery.

10. Practical scripts for protecting your boundaries

Setting boundaries when someone is in pain can feel cruel, but boundaries are one of the ways support stays sustainable. The goal is to protect your capacity without attacking the person.

When you need to leave the house: "I am feeling really overwhelmed right now, and I need to reset my own brain. I am going for a walk for thirty minutes. I will be back at 4:00."

When you cannot listen anymore: "I love you, but I cannot process any more of this worry right now. My tank is empty. Let's put a pin in this and watch a show together instead."

When you are protecting your own plans: "I know you are having a hard day, and I hate that you are struggling. I am still going to my workout class because I need it to stay grounded. I will check on you when I get back."

When they are speaking to you harshly: "I know you are panicked, but you cannot speak to me that way. I am going to step into the other room. We can try again when we are both calmer."

When you need sleep: "I care about this, and I care about you. I also need sleep tonight. I am going to rest now so I can show up better tomorrow."

11. Handling the guilt of self-care

When you finally start setting boundaries and taking time for yourself, you may feel a wave of guilt. Your brain may tell you that going to the gym while they are crying on the couch makes you selfish. It may tell you that seeing a friend while they are anxious means you are abandoning them.

That guilt can feel convincing, but it is not always telling the truth.

The truth is that if you never go to the gym, never see your friends, never sleep enough, never have silence, and never have room to be a person outside the anxiety, you will eventually resent the person you are trying to help. Resentment is often the result of ignored boundaries.

Choosing to care for yourself is not abandonment. It is preservation. You are protecting the relationship by protecting the part of you that still has patience, tenderness, humor, and steadiness to offer.

You are allowed to have needs while someone you love is struggling. Their pain does not erase your humanity.

12. Closing reflection: steadiness requires fuel

There is a common saying in caregiving circles: put your own oxygen mask on first. It is true, but it does not fully capture the daily grind of supporting someone with anxiety.

A better way to think about it is this: steadiness requires fuel.

When your loved one's internal world is chaotic, your calm, predictable response can become a lighthouse. But steadiness is not a personality trait you either have or do not have. It is a resource. It is fuel you burn every time you de-escalate a panic attack, every time you choose not to weaponize your frustration, every time you offer scaffolding instead of taking over, and every time you stay kind when you are tired.

You cannot burn fuel without refilling the tank.

When you go to the gym, see a friend, take a quiet drive, go to therapy, enforce a boundary, or protect your sleep, you are not being selfish. You are refueling. You are making sure that tomorrow, when the storm hits again, you have a better chance of responding with steadiness instead of resentment.

You owe that to them. You also owe it to yourself.

Supporting someone through anxiety should not require you to disappear. The goal is not for one person to be rescued while the other person slowly burns out. The goal is to build a life where both people have room to breathe.

Conclusion: The Long Game of Healing

The Reality of the Journey

When you first picked up this book, you may have been exhausted, confused, and desperate for something that would finally work. You wanted a sentence to say, a step to take, or a tool to use that would pull your loved one out of the spiral and bring peace back into the house.

That makes sense. When someone you love is hurting, you want relief for them. You also want relief for yourself. You want the tension to lift. You want the ordinary parts of life to feel ordinary again.

By now, you know that saving them is not the goal. Supporting them as they learn to trust themselves again is the goal.

This journey is not a sprint. It is not even a clean marathon with mile markers and a finish line. It is more like a series of unpredictable hikes through difficult terrain. Some days the weather is clear, and your loved one can walk with more confidence. Other days the storm rolls in, the freeze response takes over, and the most helpful thing you can do is stand nearby without making the storm worse.

The Transformation

Look back at the person you were before you started learning these tools. You may have been a confused helper. You may have tried to logic away their fear, answer every anxious question, push them through frozen moments, or take over the tasks they could not face. You were probably working very hard. You may have been loving them with everything you had. But sometimes, without meaning to, that help added pressure.

Now you know more.

You know that a task can look simple from the outside while feeling enormous on the inside. You know that a good day does not guarantee an easy tomorrow. You know that pressure usually increases shame, and shame usually makes movement harder. You know that support is not the same as control.

You are no longer just trying to fix what you see. You are learning to respond to what is happening underneath.

Your Greatest Contribution

The most important shift is this: your greatest contribution is not your ability to solve every problem. It is your steadiness.

Steadiness does not mean you never get tired. It does not mean you never feel frustrated, lonely, or overwhelmed. It means you are learning to pause before you add more pressure to the room. It means you are learning to lower the next step instead of raising the emotional cost. It means you are learning to hold the truth that today is just today, and a setback is not a life sentence.

When their internal world is chaotic, your calm and predictable response can become a place for their nervous system to rest. You cannot become their cure. But you can become a person who no longer accidentally feeds the spiral.

The Importance of the Done List

The Done List is simple, but its effect can be powerful. It helps the anxious brain look at evidence it would normally overlook. It turns invisible effort into something visible. It gives small wins somewhere to land.

Keep noticing the small things. Keep respecting the small steps. Keep treating basic actions as real effort when the day is heavy. Drinking water, answering one email, opening the laptop, sitting in the car outside the grocery store, resting instead of collapsing into shame - these things count.

Over time, the Done List becomes more than a list. It becomes a record of resilience. It becomes proof your loved one can return to motion, even after hard days. It becomes something they can look at when anxiety tries to convince them they have done nothing at all.

A Final Note of Hope

As you move forward, remember that your steadiness also needs care. Your patience, empathy, and calm are not endless. They are resources. Protect them. Go to the gym. See your friends. Take quiet time. Set boundaries when your tank is empty. You are not a bad support person for needing rest. You are a responsible one.

Healing from anxiety is slow and uneven. There will still be hard days. There will still be moments when old patterns return. There will still be days when both of you are tired.

But you are not starting over.

You have language now. You have a way to notice pressure before it turns into shame. You have a way to protect small wins before they disappear. You have a way to support without taking over, and a way to care for yourself without abandoning the person you love.

That is real progress.

One calmer response matters. One smaller step matters. One visible win matters. Keep building from there.

Appendix: Quick Reference Guide

The 10 Core Rules of Support

Do not feed reassurance loops. Answer the same anxious question once, then set a calm boundary so the loop does not keep growing.

Do not argue with anxiety. Validate the physical reality of fear without agreeing with the catastrophic story anxiety is telling.

Offer scaffolding, not rescuing. Break the task down and help them begin, but do not automatically take the task away.

Praise effort, not speed or perfection. The courage to attempt the task matters more than how fast or neatly it gets done.

Stop on a high note. Protect good-day energy by helping them rest before they crash.

Normalize hard days. A hard day is not proof that everything is lost. It is a hard day.

Do not call a setback a regression. Use words like pause, rest, reset, or recharging.

Do not demand proof that they are trying. If they are in a deep freeze, forcing performance for your comfort adds shame.

Use the Done List to make effort visible. Notice small wins and help preserve evidence of progress.

Protect your own capacity. You cannot offer steadiness if you are burned out.

The Done List Cheat Sheet

How to Introduce It

Try introducing the Done List during a calm moment, not during a panic attack or shutdown.

You might say:

"I know it can feel like you are not getting anything done, but I see how hard you are working just to get through the day. I want to start noticing the things that do get done, even the tiny ones, so they do not disappear."

How to Use It

Write down three to five things that were accomplished, especially the things anxiety would normally erase. The list does not have to be impressive. It has to be honest.

Drank water

Took a shower

Opened the laptop

Answered one email

Sat through panic without running from the room

Rested instead of spiraling deeper

How to Protect It

Do not turn the Done List into a scoreboard. Do not compare today's list to yesterday's list. Do not use it to prove they should do more.

If they resist it on a hard day, drop the tool and keep the spirit of it.

You might say:

"You do not have to write anything down today. Resting counts. I am just going to keep noticing the hard things you are doing."

What to Say / What Not to Say

Instead of: "There is nothing to be afraid of."

Say: "I can see how scared you are right now."

Instead of: "Just do it. It will only take five minutes."

Say: "Let us just do the very first step together."

Instead of: "You were doing so well yesterday. What happened?"

Say: "You worked really hard yesterday. It makes sense that you are tired today."

Instead of: "I cannot deal with this right now."

Say: "My tank is empty right now. I need to step away and recharge so I do not make this worse."

Essential Scripts: Hard Days

"I can see today is really heavy. You do not have to explain it."

"Let us drop the expectations for today. Drinking water and resting is enough."

"Today is just a hard day. It does not erase the progress you have made."

Essential Scripts: Good Days

"You have gotten so much done this morning. I know you want to keep going, but let us stop here."

"Let us protect your energy for tomorrow. Come sit down."

"I am really proud of the effort you put in today."

Essential Scripts: Setbacks

"Your brain is exhausted because you worked so hard yesterday. This is not a step backward."

"I know it feels like we are back at the beginning, but we are not. Your nervous system just hit a wall."

"We are going to wait right here until it settles down. There is no rush."

Essential Scripts: Caregiver Burnout

"I love you, but I cannot process more worry right now. My tank is empty."

"I am feeling overwhelmed and need to reset my own brain. I am going for a walk and I will be back soon."

"I know you are having a hard day, and I hate that you are struggling. I am still going to my workout class because I need it to stay grounded."

One-Week Practice Plan

Day 1-2: Notice reassurance loops. Do not try to fix every loop yet. Just notice how often the same anxious question comes back.

Day 3-4: Practice the boundary. Answer once, then say, "I have already answered that, and I am not going to answer it again because it feeds the panic."

Day 5-6: Practice scaffolding. When they freeze, do not take over immediately. Help them begin the smallest possible first step.

Day 7: Start the Done List. Write down three things they accomplished that required invisible effort.

Reflection Prompts for Loved Ones

What changes in me when I am rested compared to when I am burned out?

What are my warning signs that I am getting close to resentment?

Where am I most likely to take over instead of offering scaffolding?

What is one healthy outlet I need to protect this week?

What small win did I almost miss today?

What sentence could I say differently next time to lower pressure instead of raising it?

Also by Angie G. Ford

The Done List

Ease Anxiety with Small Daily Wins

You have been learning how to support someone you love through anxiety. But what about the person who is living it?

The Done List is the companion guide written for the person with anxiety themselves. It explains what anxiety actually does to daily life, why ordinary tasks can feel impossible, and how a simple shift in the way you measure your days can change your relationship with your own effort.

If the person you love is reading this book, they may need that one.

Available on Amazon.

About the Author

Angie G. Ford writes practical, compassionate books for people navigating the messy realities of life. Her work focuses on relationships, gentle productivity, and finding small ways forward on hard days. She believes that the people who stay deserve just as much support as the people they are staying for.

Book Club Discussion Guide

The Done List for Loved Ones

1. Before reading this book, how did you typically respond when someone you love was struggling with anxiety? Has anything shifted?

2. The book explains the difference between intentional avoidance and a biological freeze response. Were you surprised by any of that? How does it change the way you see past situations?

3. Which chapter or section felt most relevant to your own relationship or situation, and why?

4. The book suggests that offering logical solutions to an anxious brain often backfires. Have you experienced this? What happened?

5. What is one phrase or approach from this book you want to try the next time someone you love is in a spiral?

6. How do you personally set limits on how much support you give without burning out? Did this book change how you think about that?

7. Is there someone in your life who might benefit from reading The Done List, the companion guide written for the person with anxiety? How would you share it with them?

8. What is one mindset shift from this book you want to carry forward?

www.ingramcontent.com/pod-product-compliance
Lightning Source LLC
La Vergne TN
LVHW090524110826
845146LV00003B/971